This book belongs to:

_____

Aries Daily Horoscope 2026

Author's Note: Time set to EDT and EST Zone (UTC-4, UTC-5)

Mystic Cat
Suite 41906, 3/2237 Gold Coast HWY
Mermaid Beach, Queensland, 4218
Australia
islandauthor@hotmail.com

Contents

The 12 Zodiac Star Signs

2026

January
S	M	T	W	T	F	S
				1	2	3
4	5	6	7	8	9	10
11	12	13	14	15	16	17
18	19	20	21	22	23	24
25	26	27	28	29	30	31

February
S	M	T	W	T	F	S
1	2	3	4	5	6	7
8	9	10	11	12	13	14
15	16	17	18	19	20	21
22	23	24	25	26	27	28

March
S	M	T	W	T	F	S
1	2	3	4	5	6	7
8	9	10	11	12	13	14
15	16	17	18	19	20	21
22	23	24	25	26	27	28
29	30	31				

April
S	M	T	W	T	F	S
			1	2	3	4
5	6	7	8	9	10	11
12	13	14	15	16	17	18
19	20	21	22	23	24	25
26	27	28	29	30		

May
S	M	T	W	T	F	S
					1	2
3	4	5	6	7	8	9
10	11	12	13	14	15	16
17	18	19	20	21	22	23
24	25	26	27	28	29	30
31						

June
S	M	T	W	T	F	S
	1	2	3	4	5	6
7	8	9	10	11	12	13
14	15	16	17	18	19	20
21	22	23	24	25	26	27
28	29	30				

July
S	M	T	W	T	F	S
			1	2	3	4
5	6	7	8	9	10	11
12	13	14	15	16	17	18
19	20	21	22	23	24	25
26	27	28	29	30	31	

August
S	M	T	W	T	F	S
						1
2	3	4	5	6	7	8
9	10	11	12	13	14	15
16	17	18	19	20	21	22
23	24	25	26	27	28	29
30	31					

September
S	M	T	W	T	F	S
		1	2	3	4	5
6	7	8	9	10	11	12
13	14	15	16	17	18	19
20	21	22	23	24	25	26
27	28	29	30			

October
S	M	T	W	T	F	S
				1	2	3
4	5	6	7	8	9	10
11	12	13	14	15	16	17
18	19	20	21	22	23	24
25	26	27	28	29	30	31

November
S	M	T	W	T	F	S
1	2	3	4	5	6	7
8	9	10	11	12	13	14
15	16	17	18	19	20	21
22	23	24	25	26	27	28
29	30					

December
S	M	T	W	T	F	S
		1	2	3	4	5
6	7	8	9	10	11	12
13	14	15	16	17	18	19
20	21	22	23	24	25	26
27	28	29	30	31		

Aries Daily Horoscope 2026

The time zone is America Eastern Time EST,
or EDT during daylight saving time.

In the realm of astrology, the differences between various horoscope books for each zodiac sign stem from the intricate tapestry of celestial activity constantly unfolding in the skies. As your astrologer, my approach is to hone in on the pivotal aspects affecting a specific star sign on any given day, recognizing the uniqueness inherent in each zodiac entity.

Crafting horoscopes demands a discerning focus on the predominant astrological influences directly shaping the experiences of a particular sign. While multiple planetary configurations may be at play, I prioritize the astrological aspects that carry greater significance for a specific zodiac sign.

Delving into the ruling planets, houses, and elemental attributes associated with each sign further enriches the depth of my interpretations. This meticulous attention ensures that the guidance provided resonates authentically with the distinctive characteristics and tendencies of the intended audience.

The objective is to deliver personalized insights and advice grounded in the cosmic dynamics relevant to each zodiac sign. By emphasizing the most impactful astrological facets, I aim to assist readers in comprehending themselves more profoundly and navigating the energies surrounding them. By embracing the strengths, challenges, and opportunities inherent in each zodiac sign, my horoscope book endeavors to offer a tailored and insightful roadmap for self-discovery and growth.

Crystal

"The starry vault of heaven is in truth the open book of cosmic projection…"

—Carl Jung

JANUARY

Mon	Tue	Wed	Thu	Fri	Sat	Sun
			1	2	3	4
5	6	7	8	9	10	11
12	13	14	15	16	17	18
19	20	21	22	23	24	25
26	27	28	29	30	31	

NEW MOON

WOLF MOON

_____

_____

_____

_____

_____

_____

_____

_____

_____

_____

_____

_____

_____

_____

_____

_____

_____

_____

_____

_____

_____

29 Monday

As the Moon gracefully moves into Taurus, you may notice a shift towards a more grounded and stable emotional state. This astrological transition encourages you to seek comfort and security in your surroundings and to connect with your senses on a deeper level. Taurus' energy fosters a desire for peace and tranquility, making it an ideal time to indulge in life's simple pleasures, whether enjoying a delicious meal, spending time in nature, or surrounding yourself with beauty.

30 Tuesday

When Mercury squares Saturn, communication and decision-making can often feel like an uphill battle. You may find that your thoughts and ideas are met with resistance or obstacles, making it challenging to express yourself effectively. This aspect can bring a sense of self-doubt and a tendency to be overly critical of your abilities. Your mind may dwell on limitations and responsibilities, causing mental stress and anxiety.

31 Wednesday

On New Year's Eve, you may experience a noticeable shift in your emotional energy when the Moon ingresses into Gemini. Gemini is an air sign known for its curiosity and versatility, and this lunar placement can make you feel more mentally agile and friendly. You'll likely be in the mood to engage in conversations and connect with friends. It is when your emotions may be expressed through words, and you might find it easier to articulate them.

1 Thursday

The Sun Sextile North Node at 5:22 AM signifies a harmonious alignment between your core identity and your karmic path. This aspect suggests an opportunity to step into your authentic self-expression in a way that resonates with your soul's journey. You may find yourself feeling more confident, aligned, and in tune with your purpose. It's a favorable time for self-discovery, personal growth, and making decisions that propel you forward along your destined path.

2 Friday

At 2:27 AM, Venus forms both a sextile with the North Node and a trine with the South Node. The sextile aspect of the North Node suggests an opportunity to align your relationships and values with your soul's evolutionary journey. This aspect encourages you to embrace connections that support your growth and bring a sense of fulfillment. The trine with the South Node indicates a smooth integration of past relationship experiences and lessons into your current connections.

3 Saturday

At 5:04 AM, the Full Moon occurs, illuminating the sky with its radiant glow and marking a culmination point in the lunar cycle. This Full Moon brings heightened emotions, clarity, and awareness as the Sun opposes the Moon, highlighting the polarity between our conscious desires (Sun) and emotional needs (Moon). It's a potent time for releasing what no longer serves, acknowledging achievements, and gaining insights into areas of our lives that may require adjustment or balance.

4 Sunday

At 8:43 AM, the Moon ingresses into Leo, infusing the atmosphere with warmth, creativity, and self-expression. With the Moon in Leo, emotions become dramatic and passionate, and there's a desire to shine brightly and seek attention. This lunar transit encourages us to embrace our individuality, celebrate our talents, and express ourselves authentically. It's a time for creativity, playfulness, and taking pride in who we are. Be open to sharing with others and basking in the spotlight.

5 Monday

With Mercury in Capricorn transiting your tenth house, your approach to career and public image becomes more strategic and disciplined. This period encourages you to focus on achieving professional success through meticulous planning and clear communication. You may find yourself more willing to engage in tasks that require careful organization and attention to detail. This is a time to channel your mental energy into building a stable and prosperous professional life.

6 Tuesday

At 11:56 AM, the Moon gracefully transitions into Virgo, marking a shift towards practicality, organization, and attention to detail. Virgo is an earth sign known for its analytical nature and dedication to service. Under the influence of Virgo, you may find yourself drawn to tasks that require precision and systematic planning. This transit is an ideal period for tidying up loose ends, organizing your environment, and implementing practical solutions to everyday challenges.

7 Wednesday

Under the influence of today's energies, you may feel a strong desire to express your individuality, assert your independence, and pursue your goals with a sense of adventure. Use this energy to channel your passions into projects that excite you, explore unconventional ideas, and take calculated risks that lead to exciting opportunities for growth and expansion. Embrace the spirit of innovation and welcome unexpected breakthroughs that can propel you towards your aspirations.

8 Thursday

At 7:07 AM, as Mercury forms a sextile with the North Node and simultaneously trines the South Node, you may feel a powerful alignment between your communication style and your life's path. This harmonious aspect suggests an opportunity for you to express yourself in ways that resonate deeply with your soul's journey. Embrace this moment to make decisions and engage in conversations that propel you forward along your destined path.

9 Friday

Venus opposes Jupiter, creating a dynamic interplay between love, pleasure, and expansion. This aspect may heighten your desire for indulgence and enjoyment. You may feel drawn to seek out new experiences, explore your passions, or pursue opportunities for growth in your relationships and creative endeavors. By channeling the expansive energy of Jupiter and the harmonizing influence of Venus, you can make choices that align with your long-term happiness.

10 Saturday

At 3:42 AM, the Sun opposes Jupiter, marking a period of tension between your core identity and the planet of expansion and abundance. This aspect can bring about a clash between your sense of self and your desire for growth and opportunity. You may feel a pull towards taking risks or seeking new experiences, but there's a risk of overconfidence or exaggeration. It's essential to remain grounded and realistic in your pursuits, avoiding the temptation to overextend.

11 Sunday

At 5:55 AM, the Moon gracefully transitions into Scorpio, infusing the atmosphere with intensity, depth, and emotional transformation. During this lunar transit, you may find yourself delving into the depths of your psyche, exploring hidden truths, and experiencing powerful emotional shifts. Scorpio's influence encourages you to embrace vulnerability, confront your fears, and release what no longer serves you.

12 Monday

Mercury in Capricorn in the tenth house enhances your ability to pursue career goals with confidence and professionalism. You may feel more driven to achieve long-term professional objectives, setting clear plans and developing structured strategies to reach them. It is a time to approach your career with a practical and focused mindset. Your ability to articulate your ideas and manage your public image wisely can lead to significant progress and recognition.

13 Tuesday

At 6:34 PM, the Moon gracefully transitions into Sagittarius, infusing the atmosphere with a sense of adventure, optimism, and exploration. During this lunar transition, you may feel a strong urge to break free from routine, expand your horizons, and embrace new experiences. Sagittarius' influence encourages you to seek knowledge, broaden your perspective, and embark on exciting journeys, both physical and metaphorical.

14 Wednesday

Mercury opposes Jupiter, creating a dynamic interplay between communication, intellect, and expansion. This aspect can amplify your thoughts, ideas, and beliefs, leading to a heightened sense of optimism and enthusiasm. You may feel inclined to express yourself with confidence, share your knowledge, or engage in intellectual debates. However, it's essential to maintain a balance between optimism and realism in your communications and decision-making processes.

15 Thursday

Venus forms a harmonious sextile with Saturn, bringing stability and practicality to matters of love, relationships, and finances. This aspect encourages you to approach your commitments with dedication, responsibility, and a long-term perspective. You may find that your relationships benefit from increased maturity, loyalty, and patience during this time. Financial matters are also favored, with opportunities for creating sustainable structures and achieving financial security.

16 Friday

The Moon gracefully transitions into Capricorn, infusing the atmosphere with responsibility and practicality. During this lunar transition, you may feel a strong urge to focus on your long-term goals, establish structure and boundaries, and take concrete steps toward success. Capricorn's influence encourages you to approach tasks with discipline. Use this time to prioritize your professional ambitions, organize your priorities, and take on challenges with confidence and maturity.

17 Saturday

At 3:33 AM, Venus forms a harmonious sextile with Neptune, infusing your relationships and creative endeavors with sensitivity, compassion, and artistic inspiration. This aspect encourages you to embrace empathy, deepen emotional connections, and explore your imagination. It's a favorable time for romantic gestures, creative expression, and spiritual pursuits that nourish the soul. The energy is therapeutic, generous, and expressive.

18 Sunday

At 11:09 PM, Mercury sextiles Saturn, bringing a harmonious blend of intellect and discipline to your mental pursuits. This aspect supports focused thinking, strategic planning, and practical communication. Use this time to organize your thoughts, clarify your ideas, and establish a solid framework for achieving your goals. Embrace the power of structured thinking and responsible decision-making, knowing that your efforts are supported by the steady hand of Saturn's wisdom.

19 Monday

At 12:37 AM, Mercury forms a harmonious trine with Uranus, sparking insights, innovative ideas, and intellectual breakthroughs. This aspect enhances mental agility, creativity, and the ability to think outside the box. Embrace the opportunity to embrace change, experiment with new concepts, and communicate your ideas with clarity and originality. Trust in your intuition and embrace the excitement of discovery as you navigate uncharted territory.

20 Tuesday

Mars forms a harmonious trine with Uranus, igniting dynamic energy, innovation, and excitement. This aspect empowers you to break from constraints, embrace change, and assert your individuality with confidence. Embrace this electrifying energy to pursue your passions, explore new horizons, and welcome unexpected opportunities for growth and liberation. Shortly after, Mars sextiles Saturn, blending the energies of drive and discipline in a supportive alliance.

21 Wednesday

The Moon in Pisces envelops you in a mystical and compassionate atmosphere. During this lunar transit, you may experience heightened intuition, empathy, and a deep connection to the unseen realms. Embrace the dreamy energy of Pisces and seek solace in reflection. Allow your emotions to flow, trusting in the healing power of imagination and spiritual connection. Surrender to the gentle currents of Piscean energy as you navigate the depths of your soul.

22 Thursday

Today's astrological influences invite you to embrace transformation, take courageous action, and find the balance between self-expression and harmonious relationships. Use the energies of empowerment, initiative, and awareness to navigate challenges, pursue your passions, and cultivate meaningful connections with yourself and others. It is a time of personal and collective evolution, where you have the opportunity to embrace change and step into a chapter of growth.

23 Friday

Mars sextile Neptune infuses your actions with creativity, intuition, and spiritual insight. This aspect encourages you to channel your energy into pursuits that align with your higher ideals and innermost dreams. The synergy between ambition and imagination allows inspiration to guide your endeavors toward meaningful expression and fulfillment. Dive deep into your subconscious realms, where intuition and creativity intertwine, guiding your actions with ethereal wisdom.

24 Saturday

With the celestial bodies casting a harmonious glow, the road ahead is paved with exciting choices and decisions, helping you move past previous obstacles and embrace change. As you expand your reach into uncharted territories, you'll find invitations to explore, bringing lightness and momentum to your journey. Connecting with like-minded peers will rejuvenate your spirit and renew your surroundings. This period emphasizes improving your home and family life.

25 Sunday

At 1:05 PM, the Moon gracefully transitions into Taurus, grounding the energy and encouraging a focus on stability, comfort, and sensual pleasures. This lunar ingress invites you to indulge in life's simple pleasures, prioritize your physical well-being, and connect with the beauty of the natural world. Embrace the steady and nurturing energy of Taurus as you cultivate a sense of security and serenity in your surroundings.

26 Monday

Neptune gracefully transitions into Aries, marking a significant shift in collective consciousness and spiritual exploration. During this transit, the ethereal energy of Neptune merges with the fiery and assertive qualities of Aries, inspiring bold visions, innovative ideas, and courageous leaps of faith. Embrace the pioneering spirit of Aries as you embark on a journey of self-discovery, creative expression, and spiritual awakening.

27 Tuesday

At 3:55 PM, the Moon gracefully transitions into Gemini, infusing the atmosphere with curiosity, versatility, and social energy. During this lunar transit, you may feel a heightened sense of mental agility and a desire for communication and connection. Embrace the intellectual stimulation of Gemini by engaging in stimulating conversations, exploring new ideas, and seeking out diverse experiences. It is a favorable time for adapting to changing circumstances.

28 Wednesday

Mercury in Aquarius in the eleventh house enhances your ability to build strong and meaningful friendships and engage in community activities with innovation and determination. You may feel more driven to achieve social and community goals through clear and well-organized efforts. This is a time to approach your social interactions with a progressive and systematic mindset, allowing your attention to new ideas to foster deeper connections.

29 Thursday

The Moon tenderly transitions into Cancer, imbuing the atmosphere with nurturing, emotional depth and a desire for security. During this lunar transit, you may find yourself drawn to the comforts of home, family connections, and sentimental pursuits. Cancer's influence encourages you to honor your feelings, seek solace in familiar surroundings, and prioritize emotional well-being. Embrace the gentle nurturing energy of Cancer to cultivate deeper connections.

FEBRUARY

Mon	Tue	Wed	Thu	Fri	Sat	Sun
						1
2	3	4	5	6	7	8
9	10	11	12	13	14	15
16	17	18	19	20	21	22
23	24	25	26	27	28	

New Moon

_____

_____

_____

_____

_____

_____

_____

_____

_____

_____

_____

_____

_____

_____

_____

_____

_____

_____

_____

_____

_____

SNOW MOON

_____

_____

_____

_____

_____

_____

_____

_____

_____

_____

_____

_____

_____

_____

_____

_____

_____

_____

_____

_____

_____

30 Friday

As Venus transits through Aquarius in your eleventh house, you may find joy in exploring new social activities and hobbies that reflect your individuality. This period encourages you to step out of your comfort zone and engage with diverse social circles, fostering a sense of camaraderie and belonging. Embrace the spirit of innovation and collaboration, allowing it to guide you toward new and fulfilling experiences.

31 Saturday

At 7:09 PM, the Moon majestically transitions into Leo, igniting a sense of confidence, creativity, and self-expression. During this lunar transit, you may feel a desire to shine brightly, embrace your uniqueness, and seek out opportunities for joy and celebration. Leo's influence encourages you to express yourself authentically, follow your passions, and bask in the spotlight with grace and charisma. Embrace Leo's fiery energy to unleash your inner creativity.

1 Sunday

At 5:10 PM, the Full Moon graces the sky, illuminating the night with its radiant presence and marking the peak of the lunar cycle. This celestial event is a powerful culmination of energies, inviting you to release what no longer serves you and embrace the abundance of the present moment. The Full Moon symbolizes clarity, completion, and fulfillment, shedding light on areas of your life that may require attention or transformation.

2 Monday

The Moon gracefully transitions into Virgo, ushering in a time of practicality, organization, and attention to detail. During this lunar transit, you may feel inclined to focus on tasks that require precision and efficiency, as Virgo's influence encourages you to refine your routines and strive for perfection in your work. Embrace the analytical energy of Virgo to streamline your efforts, prioritize your responsibilities, and cultivate a sense of order in your surroundings.

3 Tuesday

As Uranus resumes its forward motion, you may experience sudden insights, breakthroughs, and a desire to break free from the limitations that have held you back. Embrace this time as an opportunity to embrace your authenticity, embrace change, and embark on a journey of self-discovery and liberation. Trust in the power of Uranus to bring unexpected opportunities for growth and evolution as you navigate the exciting terrain of the future.

4 Wednesday

With Mars in Aquarius transiting your eleventh house, your social life and community involvement are infused with dynamic energy and a drive for change. You are likely to connect with like-minded individuals who share your vision for the future and your passion for innovation. This period encourages you to actively participate in group activities and collaborative projects that make a difference. Together, you can champion causes that resonate with your ideals.

5 Thursday

The Moon gracefully transitions into Libra, infusing the atmosphere with harmony, diplomacy, and a desire for balance. During this lunar transition, you may feel drawn to seek peace, fairness, and cooperation in your interactions with others. Libra's influence encourages you to cultivate harmony in relationships. Embrace the diplomatic energy of Libra to find common ground, foster understanding, and create beauty and symmetry in your surroundings.

6 Friday

At 5:49 PM, Mercury gracefully transitions into Pisces, ushering in a period of heightened intuition, sensitivity, and imagination. During this transit, your thoughts may become more intuitive, and you may find yourself drawn to creative expression, spiritual insights, and empathy for others. Pisces' influence encourages you to listen to your inner voice, trust your instincts, and explore the realms of the subconscious mind.

7 Saturday

The Moon gracefully transitions into Scorpio, infusing the atmosphere with intensity, depth, and emotional transformation. During this lunar transit, you may find yourself drawn to explore the mysteries of life, delve into your subconscious, and seek profound truths. Scorpio's influence encourages you to embrace your inner strength, confront your fears, and undergo profound inner healing. Allow yourself to embrace vulnerability and cultivate resilience in the face of challenges.

8 Sunday

At 4:48 AM, Venus squares Uranus, creating a dynamic tension between love, beauty, and the desire for freedom and independence. This aspect may bring sudden changes or disruptions in relationships, unexpected events in matters of love or finances, or a craving for excitement and novelty. Embrace the opportunity to break free from stagnant patterns, explore new avenues of self-expression, and embrace your individuality.

9 Monday

At 7:44 AM, the Moon enters its Last Quarter phase, marking a crucial juncture in the lunar cycle for reflection, release, and reassessment. This phase encourages you to review your goals, evaluate your progress, and let go of anything that no longer serves your highest good. It's a time to release old habits, beliefs, or situations that are holding you back, making way for new beginnings in the upcoming lunar cycle.

10 Tuesday

At 2:22 AM, the Moon gracefully transitions into Sagittarius, infusing the atmosphere with optimism, adventure, and a thirst for knowledge. During this lunar transit, you may feel inspired to explore new horizons, expand your beliefs, and seek out experiences that broaden your perspective. Sagittarius' influence encourages you to embrace spontaneity and diversity as you follow your sense of wanderlust.

11 Wednesday

With the stars in your favor, a dynamic period is on the horizon, filled with choices that enhance your journey. Stay open to the exciting leads that cross your path, as they promise significant improvements. This lively and productive phase invites thrilling changes and opportunities, enriching your world. Embrace the grand entrance of something unique that sparks a journey of inspiration and exhilaration. New endeavors will ignite your creativity and nurture your talents.

12 Thursday

At 1:17 AM, Mercury opposes the South Node, creating a dynamic tension between your past and present communication styles and thought patterns. This aspect may bring up old beliefs, habits, or ways of thinking that no longer serve your growth and evolution. It's a time to reflect on the past and release any outdated perspectives or mental patterns that are holding you back from embracing new possibilities and moving forward with clarity and purpose.

13 Friday

At 7:37 PM, Saturn gracefully transitions into Aries, marking a significant shift in the cosmic landscape and collective consciousness. As Saturn moves into the fiery and assertive sign of Aries, it brings a focus on individuality, initiative, and self-discovery. This transit prompts you to take a more proactive approach to achieving your goals, asserting your independence, and overcoming challenges with courage and determination.

14 Saturday

As the cosmos gently shifts, nurturing the foundations of your life creates a balanced and stable environment ripe for growth. New leads will spark thoughts of expansion, while a forthcoming learning opportunity will become a source of inspiration. This period brings both challenges and advancements for your career, urging you to develop your skills and move towards greener pastures. Stay open to growth, as it allows you to step into an extended time of realizing your dreams.

15 Sunday

The Moon transitions into Aquarius, infusing the atmosphere with innovation, humanitarianism, and a spirit of individuality. During this lunar transition, you may feel drawn to unconventional ideas, progressive causes, and collaborative efforts that promote social change. Aquarius' influence encourages you to embrace your unique perspective, celebrate diversity, and cultivate connections with like-minded visionaries who share your passion for creating a better world.

16 Monday

The Sun forms a challenging square aspect with Uranus, heralding a period of potential disruption, rebellion, and unexpected change. This aspect may bring sudden events, disruptions, or the urge to break free from restrictions and embrace independence. It's a time to expect the unexpected and remain flexible in the face of uncertainty. Embrace the opportunity to innovate, experiment, and explore new possibilities, but be mindful of impulsive actions or rebellious behavior.

17 Tuesday

At 7:02 AM, the New Moon graces the sky, marking the beginning of a new lunar cycle and a powerful opportunity for setting intentions, initiating projects, and planting seeds for the future. This lunar phase invites you to connect with your inner desires, visualize your goals, and take proactive steps toward manifesting your dreams. Embrace the energy of new beginnings and fresh starts as you embark on a journey of growth, transformation, and self-discovery.

18 Wednesday

At 10:54 AM, the Sun gracefully transitions into Pisces, marking a shift in focus towards intuition, compassion, and spiritual exploration. During this solar transit, you may feel more attuned to your emotions, imagination, and inner world. Pisces' influence encourages you to embrace empathy, creativity, and a deeper connection to the universal energies that surround you. It's a time to trust your intuition, explore your dreams, and tap into your inner wisdom.

19 Thursday

The Moon in Aries infuses the atmosphere with courage, vitality, and a pioneering spirit. During this lunar transit, you feel a surge of energy and enthusiasm, propelling you towards new beginnings and exciting adventures. Aries' influence encourages you to assert yourself boldly, take decisive action, and pursue goals with passion and determination. Embrace the fiery energy of Aries as you embark on a journey of self-discovery, independence, and personal growth.

20 Friday

The astrological climate beams new opportunities your way, ushering in a busy and exciting time filled with developments that enable progress. Focusing on developing your social life will attract rewarding outcomes. With invitations and possibilities on the rise, life picks up pace, promoting growing friendships. Supportive energy creates a robust environment, with increasing choices adding a sweet flavor, preparing you for new adventures shared with friends.

21 Saturday

At 6:31 PM, the Moon gracefully transitions into Taurus, infusing the atmosphere with stability, sensuality, and a desire for comfort. During this lunar transit, you may feel a strong need for security, indulgence in life's pleasures, and a connection to the natural world. Taurus' influence encourages you to slow down, savor the present moment, and prioritize your physical and emotional well-being. It's a time for grounding yourself and appreciating the beauty of the world.

22 Sunday

At 3:01 PM, Venus forms a harmonious trine aspect with Jupiter, creating a beautiful alignment of love, abundance, and expansion. This celestial combination brings forth a sense of joy, optimism, and generosity in matters of love, relationships, and finances. It's a time of increased harmony, luck, and opportunities for growth and prosperity. You may feel more open-hearted, friendly, and inclined to indulge in life's pleasures.

23 Monday

The Moon in Gemini infuses the atmosphere with curiosity, adaptability, and sociability. During this lunar transit, you may feel a desire for communication, intellectual stimulation, and variety in your experiences. Gemini's influence encourages you to engage in lively conversations, exchange ideas, and explore new interests with enthusiasm. Embrace the versatility of Gemini to embrace change, connect with others, and cultivate a sense of playfulness and spontaneity.

24 Tuesday

At 7:28 AM, the Moon reaches its First Quarter phase, marking a pivotal moment in the lunar cycle for taking action and overcoming challenges. This lunar aspect invites you to assess your progress since the New Moon and make any necessary adjustments to your goals or plans. It's a time to push forward with determination, courage, and initiative as you work towards manifesting your intentions into reality. Embrace the energy of the First Quarter Moon to take decisive action.

25 Wednesday

Today's graceful celestial guidance lets you integrate change sustainably to achieve a grounded foundation from which to grow your life outwardly. As things turn a corner, you soon get busy in a dynamic environment. A new option on offer advances your life forward, creating a heightened sense of security that gives you the stability needed to grow your life. The cosmic energies support your path to stability and progress.

26 Thursday

Mercury turns retrograde, marking a period of introspection, review, and reevaluation in communication, travel, and technology. During this retrograde phase, you may experience delays, misunderstandings, or challenges in communication and decision-making. It's a time to revisit old projects, reflect on past experiences, and resolve any lingering issues or miscommunications. Embrace the opportunity to reassess your plans and clarify your intentions.

MARCH

Mon	Tue	Wed	Thu	Fri	Sat	Sun
						1
2	3	4	5	6	7	8
9	10	11	12	13	14	15
16	17	18	19	20	21	22
23	24	25	26	27	28	29
30	31					

NEW MOON

_____

_____

_____

_____

_____

_____

_____

_____

_____

_____

_____

_____

_____

_____

_____

_____

_____

_____

_____

_____

_____

WORM MOON

_____

_____

_____

_____

_____

_____

_____

_____

_____

_____

_____

_____

_____

_____

_____

_____

_____

_____

_____

27 Friday

At 7:32 AM, the Sun opposes the South Node, creating a dynamic tension between your current path and past patterns or karmic influences. This aspect may bring up challenges or conflicts related to your sense of identity, purpose, and direction in life. It's a time to confront and release any outdated beliefs, behaviors, or attachments that are holding you back from fully embracing your potential and moving forward.

28 Saturday

The Moon boldly transitions into Leo, infusing the atmosphere with a sense of confidence, creativity, and self-expression. During this lunar transit, you may feel a desire to shine brightly, express yourself boldly, and seek out opportunities for recognition and applause. Leo's influence encourages you to embrace your inner spark, share your talents with the world, and cultivate a sense of pride in who you are. It's a time for playfulness, romance, and celebrating the joys of life.

1 Sunday

As Venus moves through Pisces in your twelfth house, you may feel a stronger desire to refine your introspective and spiritual pursuits. Embrace the opportunity to engage in thoughtful and imaginative conversations and practices. This period invites you to manifest your spiritual goals with clarity and purpose, allowing you to achieve greater self-awareness and inner peace. Exploring artistic or meditative practices can deepen your spiritual journey.

2 Monday

Mars transitions into Pisces, infusing the atmosphere with a blend of sensitivity, intuition, and spirituality. During this transit, your actions may be guided by empathy, compassion, and a desire for transcendence. Pisces' influence encourages you to harness the power of your imagination, trust your instincts, and pursue your goals with purpose and divine inspiration. It's a time for creative exploration, spiritual growth, and embracing the interconnectedness of all beings.

3 Tuesday

The celestial Full Moon event symbolizes a time of heightened emotions, clarity, and release. As the Moon reaches its peak in brightness, it invites you to reflect on your intentions set during the New Moon and acknowledge the progress you've made since then. Embrace the illuminating energy of the Full Moon to let go of what no longer serves you, celebrate your achievements, and embrace the transformative power of surrender.

4 Wednesday

The Moon gracefully transitions into Libra, bringing a sense of harmony, diplomacy, and balance to the atmosphere. During this lunar transit, you may feel inclined to seek peace, fairness, and cooperation in your relationships and surroundings. Libra's influence encourages you to cultivate harmony in your interactions, appreciate beauty and aesthetics, and strive for fairness and justice. It's a time for diplomacy, compromise, and finding common ground with others.

5 Thursday

The Sun forms a harmonious trine aspect with Jupiter, amplifying feelings of optimism, abundance, and expansion. This celestial alignment brings a sense of joy, confidence, and opportunity, encouraging you to embrace life. It's a favorable time for setting ambitious goals, taking calculated risks, and exploring new horizons. With the radiant energy of the Sun and the expansive influence of Jupiter working together, you may experience good fortune, growth, and success.

6 Friday

At 5:47 AM, Venus gracefully transitions into Aries, marking a shift towards a more assertive, passionate, and spontaneous approach to love, beauty, and values. During this transit, you may feel a strong desire for independence, excitement, and individual expression in your relationships and creative endeavors. Aries' influence encourages you to pursue your passions with courage, take initiative in matters of the heart, and embrace your inner fire and vitality.

7 Saturday

With the Sun in Pisces transiting your twelfth house, your focus on introspection and spiritual growth becomes more intuitive and deeply personal. This period encourages you to approach your inner world with a sense of compassion and understanding. You may find yourself more interested in exploring the hidden aspects of your psyche and seeking out spiritual practices that promote healing. This is a time to channel your energy into quiet reflection and inner work.

8 Sunday

With Mars in Pisces transiting your twelfth house, your approach to introspection and spirituality becomes more intuitive and transformative. This period encourages you to explore your inner world with compassion and depth. You may find yourself more willing to confront hidden fears and unresolved issues, leading to profound healing and spiritual growth. This is a time to channel your energy into practices that promote inner peace and self-discovery.

9 Monday

At 1:22 AM, Mercury forms a harmonious trine aspect with Jupiter, amplifying your mental faculties, communication skills, and opportunities for expansion. This aspect enhances your ability to think big, express yourself with confidence, and embrace new ideas and opportunities. It's a favorable time for learning, teaching, traveling, and engaging in philosophical or spiritual pursuits. Embrace the expansive energy of Mercury trine Jupiter to broaden your horizons.

10 Tuesday

At 2:52 AM, Venus forms a harmonious sextile aspect with Pluto, infusing your relationships and creative endeavors with depth, passion, and transformative energy. This aspect invites you to explore the deeper layers of intimacy, allowing for profound emotional connections and personal growth. You may experience a sense of empowerment in your relationships, as well as a heightened ability to heal and release old wounds.

11 Wednesday

At 5:39 AM, the Moon reaches its Last Quarter phase, marking a pivotal moment in the lunar cycle for reflection, release, and completion. This lunar aspect invites you to evaluate your progress, identify what no longer serves your highest good, and make adjustments as you prepare for the next phase of growth. It's a time to release any lingering doubts, fears, or limitations that may be holding you back and to embrace the wisdom gained from your experiences.

12 Thursday

At 12:07 AM, the Moon gracefully transitions into Capricorn, bringing a sense of practicality, ambition, and determination to the forefront. During this lunar transit, you may feel more focused on your goals, responsibilities, and long-term plans. Capricorn's influence encourages you to approach tasks with discipline, perseverance, and a strategic mindset. It's a favorable time for setting realistic goals, organizing your priorities, and taking concrete steps toward success.

13 Friday

At 4:52 PM, Mars opposes the South Node, creating a dynamic tension between assertiveness, action, and past karmic patterns. This aspect may bring up conflicts or challenges related to asserting your willpower or pursuing your desires in alignment with your soul's evolutionary journey. You may feel a pull towards familiar patterns or behaviors that no longer serve your highest good, prompting you to confront any lingering issues from the past.

14 Saturday

The Aquarius' Moon influence encourages you to embrace your individuality, think outside the box, and champion causes that promote collective progress and equality. It's a favorable time for engaging in group activities, brainstorming creative ideas, and fostering a sense of community with like-minded individuals. Embrace the progressive energy of Aquarius as you explore new perspectives, advocate for positive change, and celebrate the diversity of human experience.

15 Sunday

Sun in Pisces in the twelfth house enhances your ability to navigate the realms of the unconscious and connect with the divine. You may feel more driven to explore new ways of accessing your inner wisdom and understanding the mysteries of your soul. Embrace this opportunity to engage in practices such as meditation, dream work, and spiritual retreats that allow you to connect with your inner self. Your compassionate approach to introspection will help you release old wounds.

16 Monday

At 7:15 PM, the Moon gracefully transitions into Pisces, infusing the atmosphere with sensitivity, imagination, and compassion. During this lunar transition, you may feel more attuned to your emotions, dreams, and the subtle energies around you. Pisces' influence encourages you to embrace your intuition, creativity, and spiritual connection. It's a time for introspection, artistic expression, and tapping into the collective unconscious.

17 Tuesday

At 5:00 PM, Mercury forms an opposition aspect with the South Node, creating tension between your current thoughts, communication style, and past patterns or karmic influences. This aspect may bring up challenges related to old habits of thinking, outdated beliefs, or unresolved issues from the past. You may find yourself confronted with misunderstandings, communication breakdowns, or difficulties in expressing yourself effectively.

18 Wednesday

At 12:08 PM, Venus forms a challenging square aspect with Jupiter, creating a tension between love, pleasure, and indulgence, and the need for moderation and balance. This aspect may bring about feelings of extravagance, overconfidence, or a tendency to overextend oneself in matters of love, finances, or social activities. It's essential to be mindful of excesses and avoid making impulsive decisions or taking undue risks during this time.

19 Thursday

At 12:03 AM, the Moon boldly enters Aries, ushering in a surge of dynamic energy, courage, and initiative. During this lunar transit, you may feel a strong sense of assertiveness, drive, and a desire to take action. Aries' influence encourages you to embrace your individuality, assert your needs, and pursue your goals with enthusiasm and determination. It's a time for initiating new projects, asserting yourself in relationships, and embracing challenges with confidence.

20 Friday

The Vernal March Equinox marks the official beginning of spring in the Northern Hemisphere. This astronomical event occurs when the tilt of the Earth's axis is neither inclined away from nor towards the Sun, resulting in nearly equal lengths of day and night. The Equinox symbolizes a time of balance, renewal, and awakening as nature comes to life after the winter months. It's a decisive moment to embrace the energy of growth, beginnings, and the promise of brighter days.

21 Saturday

At 2:35 AM, the Moon gracefully transitions into Taurus, infusing the atmosphere with a sense of stability, comfort, and sensual pleasure. During this lunar transit, you may feel a desire to indulge in life's simple pleasures, such as good food, relaxation, and physical comforts. Taurus' influence encourages you to cultivate a sense of security and stability in your surroundings, prioritize self-care, and connect with nature's abundance.

22 Sunday

At 8:49 PM, Mercury opposes the South Node, marking a period of tension and reflection regarding communication, thought patterns, and past influences. This aspect may bring up challenges related to outdated beliefs, habits, or communication styles that no longer serve your highest good. You may find yourself confronting unresolved issues from the past or experiencing misunderstandings in your interactions with others.

23 Monday

At 4:18 AM, the Moon gracefully transitions into Gemini, ushering in a time of curiosity, versatility, and sociability. During this lunar transit, you may feel a heightened sense of mental agility, a desire for intellectual stimulation, and a need for social interaction. Gemini's influence encourages you to engage in lively conversations, explore new ideas, and connect with others through communication and exchange of information.

24 Tuesday

Today's astrological influences highlight the balance between discipline and creativity, responsibility and self-expression. Find ways to integrate these energies harmoniously, honoring your commitments and responsibilities while also nurturing your creative spirit with opportunities for joy and self-expression. Trust Your abilities, stay true to your passions, and embrace the opportunities for growth and fulfillment that arise during this dynamic cosmic dance.

25 Wednesday

At 6:33 AM, the Moon transitions into Cancer, infusing the atmosphere with emotional sensitivity, nurturing energy, and a desire for security and comfort. During this lunar transit, you may find yourself drawn to activities that evoke feelings of warmth, closeness, and familiarity. Cancer's influence encourages you to prioritize your emotional well-being, nurture your relationships, and create a safe and supportive environment for yourself and others.

26 Thursday

Venus in Aries in the first house enhances your ability to initiate new relationships and take the lead in social situations. You may feel more driven to assert your needs and desires, making it easier to pursue your personal goals with determination. This is a time to explore new ways of presenting yourself and to take risks in your self-expression. Your ability to attract attention and inspire others can lead to exciting opportunities and personal growth.

27 Friday

The Moon gracefully transitions into Leo, infusing the atmosphere with warmth, creativity, and a desire for self-expression. During this lunar transition, you may feel more outgoing, confident, and eager to shine in the spotlight. Leo's influence encourages you to embrace your unique talents, passions, and individuality and to share your light with the world. Embrace Leo's vibrant energy as you express yourself authentically and boldly pursue your creative endeavors.

28 Saturday

At 6:10 PM, Saturn forms a harmonious sextile aspect with Pluto, aligning the energies of structure and transformation in a powerful and supportive manner. This aspect brings a sense of stability, discipline, and long-term planning to the transformative processes that Pluto represents. You may find that you have the determination, resilience, and practicality needed to navigate profound changes in your life with grace and maturity.

29 Sunday

At 3:33 PM, the Moon gracefully transitions into Virgo, ushering in a period of practicality, organization, and attention to detail. During this lunar transit, you may feel inclined to focus on tasks that require precision and efficiency, seeking to improve systems and streamline processes. Virgo's influence encourages you to pay attention to the finer points, analyze situations critically, and strive for perfection in your endeavors.

APRIL

Mon	Tue	Wed	Thu	Fri	Sat	Sun
		1	2	3	4	5
6	7	8	9	10	11	12
13	14	15	16	17	18	19
20	21	22	23	24	25	26
27	28	29	30			

New Moon

PINK MOON

30 Monday

At 12:02 PM, Venus gracefully enters Taurus, infusing the atmosphere with sensual pleasures, stability, and a deep appreciation for the beauty of life. During this transit, you may find yourself drawn to the finer things in life, indulging in creature comforts and seeking out experiences that bring you joy and satisfaction. Venus in Taurus encourages you to cultivate a sense of abundance, connect with nature, and nurture your relationships with patience and devotion.

31 Tuesday

At 10:51 PM, the Moon gracefully transitions into Libra, infusing the atmosphere with harmony, diplomacy, and a desire for balance. During this lunar transit, you may feel more inclined to seek peace and harmony in your relationships and surroundings. Libra's influence encourages cooperation, compromise, and a focus on fairness and justice. It's a favorable time for socializing, cultivating connections, and finding common ground with others.

1 Wednesday

Welcome the Full Moon, a potent celestial event that illuminates the night sky with its radiant glow. This phase of the lunar cycle marks a culmination point, where intentions set during the New Moon come to fruition, and emotions reach a peak. The Full Moon in Libra emphasizes themes of balance, relationships, and harmony. It invites you to reflect on the balance between your needs and the needs of others and to seek harmony in your connections with those around you.

2 Thursday

With Mercury in Pisces transiting your twelfth house, your approach to introspection and spirituality becomes more intuitive. This period encourages you to explore your inner world and address subconscious issues with a compassionate and visionary approach. You may find yourself more willing to engage in activities that require a holistic and empathetic approach. This is a time to channel your mental energy into creating inner strength and profound self-discovery.

3 Friday

At 6:38 PM, Venus forms a challenging square aspect with Pluto, bringing intensity and power struggles to relationships and financial matters. This aspect may evoke feelings of possessiveness, jealousy, or control, leading to potential conflicts or confrontations. It's essential to approach situations with honesty, integrity, and a willingness to address underlying issues to foster healing and transformation in relationships.

4 Saturday

With the Sun in Aries transiting your first house, you are entering a period of heightened energy and self-expression. This placement brings a surge of confidence and a strong desire to assert your individuality. You may feel more driven to take bold actions and make decisions that reflect your true self. This is a time to channel your energy into personal initiatives and projects that allow you to showcase your talents and strengths.

5 Sunday

The Sun forms a tense square aspect with Jupiter, creating a dynamic and potentially challenging energy. This aspect may bring about a clash between optimism and overconfidence, leading to exaggerated expectations or a tendency to overextend oneself. While Jupiter's influence can inspire growth and expansion, the square aspect from the Sun may highlight areas where moderation and discipline are needed to avoid overdoing things.

6 Monday

At 5:47 AM, Venus forms a harmonious sextile aspect with the North Node, followed by a trine aspect with the South Node, aligning the realms of love, harmony, and destiny. These aspects suggest a profound alignment between your relationships, values, and karmic path. The sextile with the North Node offers an opportunity to deepen connections, attract positive relationships, and align with your soul's purpose.

7 Tuesday

Venus in Taurus in the second house enhances your ability to attract financial opportunities and manage your resources with care and diligence. You may feel more driven to achieve economic stability through patient and well-considered actions. This is a time to approach your finances with a calm and determined mindset. Your ability to value quality over quantity and to make prudent investments can lead to increased financial security and satisfaction.

8 Wednesday

Embrace the dynamic interplay between Capricorn Moon's grounded practicality and Mars-Uranus' innovative spirit as you navigate the day. Use the disciplined energy of Capricorn to focus your efforts and the bold, innovative influence of Mars sextile Uranus to infuse your actions with creativity and excitement. It's a time for strategic action, calculated risk-taking, and embracing opportunities for growth and transformation.

9 Thursday

Mars charges into Aries, its home sign, heralding a surge of boldness, determination, and raw energy. This astrological shift ignites a fiery enthusiasm and a fierce desire to conquer new horizons. With Mars in Aries, you're propelled forward with a sense of urgency, ready to embrace challenges and pursue passions with unyielding determination. This transit empowers you to tap into your inner warrior, unleashing your drive and courageously pushing boundaries.

10 Friday

At 12:52 AM, you experience the Moon's Last Quarter, a phase that signifies a time of reflection, release, and preparation for new beginnings. This lunar event prompts you to review your goals, assess your progress, and let go of anything that no longer serves your highest good, allowing space for fresh opportunities to emerge. Embrace this phase as a chance to release old patterns, beliefs, or habits that may be holding you back, paving the way for growth and renewal.

11 Saturday

Saturn in Aries in the first house enhances your ability to take charge of your life and pursue your goals with unwavering commitment. You may feel more focused on achieving long-term objectives and setting clear boundaries. This is a time to approach your personal development with a structured and systematic mindset. Your ability to overcome obstacles with determination can lead to significant achievements and individual empowerment.

12 Sunday

With Neptune in Aries transiting your first house, your sense of self and personal identity becomes intertwined with a dreamy and visionary quality. You may find yourself drawn to idealistic pursuits and inspired by a sense of boundless potential. This period encourages you to express your individuality in unique and imaginative ways, blending your assertive nature with a touch of mysticism. Embrace this opportunity to explore new aspects of your identity.

APRIL

13 Monday

Venus forms a harmonious sextile aspect with Jupiter, aligning the realms of love, abundance, and expansion. This celestial combination fosters feelings of optimism and generosity in relationships and financial matters. It's a favorable time for socializing, enjoying life's pleasures, and indulging in leisure activities. You may experience a sense of abundance and gratitude, attracting positive experiences and opportunities that uplift your spirits and expand your horizons.

14 Tuesday

Mercury forms a dynamic sextile aspect with Uranus, sparking innovative thinking, original ideas, and sudden insights. This celestial alignment encourages you to embrace change and explore unconventional solutions to problems. Under this influence, your mind is open to new possibilities, and you may feel inspired to communicate your ideas with clarity and enthusiasm. It's a favorable time for brainstorming, experimenting, and embracing spontaneity.

15 Wednesday

The Moon in your sign infuses the atmosphere with fiery energy, enthusiasm, and a pioneering spirit. During this lunar transit, you may feel a surge of vitality, motivation, and assertiveness as Aries encourages you to take action and pursue your goals with determination. It's a time for embracing new beginnings, seizing opportunities, and asserting your individuality with confidence. Under the influence of the Aries Moon, you may feel inspired to tackle challenges head-on.

16 Thursday

Mars forms a harmonious sextile aspect with Pluto, blending the energies of assertiveness and transformation constructively. This celestial alignment empowers you with resilience, determination, and purpose. You may find yourself drawn to pursue your ambitions with unwavering focus and intensity, fueled by a desire for growth and empowerment. Under this influence, you can tap into your inner strength to create positive change.

APRIL

17 Friday

At 7:52 AM, welcome the New Moon, a potent lunar phase marking the beginning of a lunar cycle and a time of fresh starts, intentions, and opportunities. Under this celestial influence, you are encouraged to set intentions for the future, plant seeds of growth, and embark on new beginnings aligned with your deepest desires and aspirations. It's a decisive moment for introspection, manifestation, and laying the groundwork for your dreams to take root and flourish.

18 Saturday

At 4:35 PM, Mercury forms a harmonious sextile aspect with Pluto, creating a potent alignment of mental clarity, depth, and transformation. This celestial event empowers you to delve beneath the surface, uncover hidden truths, and engage in meaningful introspection. Under this influence, your mind is sharp, intuitive, and capable of penetrating insights, allowing you to navigate complex situations with finesse and understanding.

19 Sunday

At 12:17 PM, the Moon transitions into Gemini, infusing the atmosphere with curiosity, adaptability, and a desire for intellectual stimulation. In Gemini, the Moon encourages you to embrace variety, socialize, and engage in lively communication. It's a favorable time for learning, networking, and exploring new ideas. Embrace the versatile energy of the Gemini Moon as you seek out new experiences, connect with others, and satisfy your intellectual curiosity.

20 Monday

Mars in Aries in the first house enhances your ability to initiate new projects and assert yourself with courage and enthusiasm. You may feel more driven to achieve personal goals through direct and energetic efforts. This is a time to explore your passions and express your desires in a way that aligns with your authentic self. Embrace this opportunity to lead with confidence and determination, creating a path that is both exciting and fulfilling.

21 Tuesday

At 1:00 PM, the Moon tenderly transitions into Cancer, infusing the atmosphere with sensitivity, nurturing energy, and a deep connection to the emotional realm. In Cancer, the Moon encourages you to prioritize self-care, nurture your loved ones, and create a sense of comfort and security in your surroundings. You may find yourself more attuned to your feelings and those of others, seeking solace in familiar spaces and cherished memories.

22 Wednesday

With Mercury in Aries transiting your first house, your communication style becomes more direct and assertive. This period encourages you to express yourself with confidence and clarity, allowing your thoughts to be conveyed with enthusiasm and vigor. You may find yourself more willing to take the lead in conversations and to initiate new ideas. This is a time to channel your mental energy into personal projects that benefit from a bold and proactive approach.

23 Thursday

At 3:41 PM, the Moon majestically transitions into Leo, infusing the atmosphere with warmth, creativity, and a desire for self-expression. In Leo, the Moon encourages you to embrace your individuality, shine brightly, and express yourself with confidence and enthusiasm. You may feel a surge of creativity and passion, inspiring you to pursue your hobbies, showcase your talents, or take center stage in your endeavors.

24 Friday

In Gemini, Venus encourages you to embrace variety, diversity, and intellectual stimulation in your relationships and pleasures. You may find yourself more inclined to engage in witty banter, explore different interests, and seek out new experiences that stimulate your mind and senses. It's a favorable time for networking, socializing, and connecting with others through engaging conversation and shared interests.

25 Saturday

The Sun forms a challenging square aspect with Pluto, marking a potent alignment that may bring power struggles, intensity, and transformation to the forefront. This celestial event prompts you to confront deep-seated issues, face fears, and dismantle obstacles that stand in the way of your personal growth. While this aspect can be intense, it also offers an opportunity for profound inner healing and empowerment as you embrace change and release what no longer serves you.

26 Sunday

At 1:42 PM, a harmonious aspect forms as Venus sextiles Neptune, infusing the atmosphere with dreamy, romantic, and compassionate energy. This celestial alignment encourages you to connect with your intuition, express your creativity, and nurture your relationships with empathy and sensitivity. You may feel inspired to indulge in artistic pursuits, spend time in nature, or engage in acts of kindness and compassion towards others.

27 Monday

At 9:19 AM, the Sun forms both a sextile aspect with the North Node and a trine aspect with the South Node, marking a significant alignment that influences your path forward and your past experiences simultaneously. The sextile with the North Node signifies a harmonious connection with your karmic path and destiny. It presents an opportunity for growth, personal development, and alignment with your life's purpose.

28 Tuesday

In Libra, the Moon encourages you to seek fairness, cooperation, and mutual understanding in your interactions with others. You may find yourself more inclined to seek out companionship, engage in social activities, and strive for peace and harmony in your environment. It's a favorable time for compromise, negotiation, and finding common ground in any conflicts or disagreements that may arise.

29 Wednesday

Venus square the South Node indicates that you may be confronted with past patterns, attachments, or karmic influences that hinder your ability to move forward in your relationships and values. This aspect encourages you to release outdated beliefs, behaviors, or connections that no longer serve your highest good, allowing you to break free from the constraints of the past and embrace new possibilities for growth and fulfillment.

30 Thursday

The Moon transitions into Scorpio, infusing the atmosphere with intensity, depth, and emotional transformation. In Scorpio, the Moon encourages you to delve beneath the surface and explore the depths of your psyche. You may find yourself drawn to introspection, uncovering hidden truths, and experiencing heightened emotional sensitivity. This lunar ingress invites you to embrace the shadow aspects of yourself and others, facilitating profound healing and regeneration.

MAY

Mon	Tue	Wed	Thu	Fri	Sat	Sun
				1	2	3
4	5	6	7	8	9	10
11	12	13	14	15	16	17
18	19	20	21	22	23	24
25	26	27	28	29	30	31

NEW MOON

FLOWER MOON

MAY

1 Friday

At 1:24 PM, the sky illuminates with the radiant glow of the Full Moon, marking a peak moment in the lunar cycle when emotions are heightened and intentions come to fruition. This celestial event invites you to embrace illumination, clarity, and culmination in various areas of your life. It's a time to reflect on your achievements, celebrate your progress, and release anything that no longer serves your highest good. The Full Moon encourages you to honor your emotions.

2 Saturday

Mercury enters Taurus, infusing your thoughts and communication style with practicality, stability, and a focus on the tangible world. In Taurus, Mercury encourages you to slow down, savor the moment, and approach matters with patience and deliberation. You may find yourself more attuned to your physical senses, preferring to communicate straightforwardly and methodically. This transit favors concrete thinking, financial planning, and attention to detail.

3 Sunday

At 2:33 AM, the Moon gracefully transitions into Sagittarius, infusing the atmosphere with a sense of adventure, optimism, and expansiveness. In Sagittarius, the Moon encourages you to embrace spontaneity, seek out new experiences, and explore the world with a spirit of enthusiasm and curiosity. You may feel a heightened sense of freedom and independence, inspiring you to break free from routine and embrace opportunities for growth and exploration.

MAY

4 Monday

Mars forms a challenging square aspect with Jupiter, bringing a surge of energy, ambition, and enthusiasm that can be both empowering and potentially overwhelming. This celestial alignment encourages you to take action toward your goals with confidence and assertiveness. Still, it also warns against excessive impulsiveness, overconfidence, or taking on more than you can handle. You may feel a desire to push beyond limitations and pursue your ambitions with vigor.

5 Tuesday

At 3:06 PM, the Moon transitions into Capricorn, marking a shift towards a more disciplined, pragmatic, and goal-oriented emotional state. In Capricorn, the Moon encourages you to take a structured and responsible approach to your feelings and actions, prioritizing long-term success and stability. This lunar transit emphasizes the need for practicality, determination, and perseverance in pursuing your ambitions and goals.

6 Wednesday

The sextile with the North Node invites you to explore new ideas, communicate with clarity and authenticity, and embrace opportunities for personal and intellectual expansion that align with your soul's purpose. Meanwhile, the opposition with the South Node encourages you to release outdated thought patterns or beliefs. It's a favorable time for introspection, self-reflection, and letting go of baggage that may be holding you back from realizing your full potential.

7 Thursday

With Mercury in Taurus transiting your second house, your approach to finances and material possessions becomes more practical and methodical. This period encourages you to manage your resources with a focus on long-term stability and security. You may find yourself more interested in exploring reliable and steady ways of earning and managing money. It is a time to channel your mental energy into building financial security through careful planning and persistence.

8 Friday

At 3:27 AM, the Moon gracefully transitions into Aquarius, ushering in a period characterized by innovation, individuality, and humanitarian ideals. In Aquarius, the Moon encourages you to embrace your uniqueness, think outside the box, and seek out unconventional solutions to challenges. You may feel a heightened sense of independence and a desire to break free from societal norms or restrictions, opting instead to follow your path and express your authentic self freely.

9 Saturday

The Moon reaches its Last Quarter phase, marking a pivotal moment in the lunar cycle. The Last Quarter Moon encourages you to evaluate your progress, acknowledge any obstacles or challenges you've encountered, and determine what adjustments need to be made to align with your goals and intentions. It's a potent opportunity to release old patterns, habits, or beliefs that may be holding you back and to make space for new growth and opportunities in the upcoming lunar cycle.

10 Sunday

At 10:13 PM, the Sun forms a harmonious sextile aspect with Jupiter, creating a potent alignment that brings optimism, growth, and expansion. This celestial event enhances your confidence, generosity, and sense of abundance, inspiring you to pursue opportunities for personal and spiritual growth. You may feel a renewed sense of enthusiasm for your goals and aspirations, as well as a willingness to take calculated risks in pursuit of your dreams.

11 Monday

With Venus in Gemini transiting your third house, your communication style and intellectual pursuits become more harmonious and dynamic. You may find yourself focusing on practical ways to express your ideas with clarity and enthusiasm. This period encourages you to embrace a lively and adaptable approach to learning and communication, blending your natural curiosity with a desire for social interaction and intellectual growth.

12 Tuesday

The Moon shifts into Aries, igniting a fiery and dynamic energy that encourages assertiveness, initiative, and spontaneity. In Aries, the Moon inspires you to take action and pursue your passions. You may feel a surge of energy and enthusiasm, propelling you to embark on new beginnings and pursue your goals with determination and vigor. This lunar transit encourages you to trust your instincts, embrace your inner warrior, and fearlessly pursue what sets your soul on fire.

13 Wednesday

Mercury forms a harmonious sextile aspect with Jupiter, creating a celestial alignment that enhances communication, learning, and expansive thinking. This aspect fosters a sense of optimism, curiosity, and intellectual growth, inspiring you to explore new ideas, concepts, and possibilities with enthusiasm and openness. You may find yourself more inclined to engage in meaningful conversations, share your knowledge and wisdom, or seek opportunities for learning and development.

14 Thursday

At 10:31 PM, the Moon gracefully transitions into Taurus, marking a shift in the emotional landscape towards stability, comfort, and sensual pleasures. In Taurus, the Moon encourages you to seek security, indulge in creature comforts, and connect with the beauty of the physical world. You may find yourself drawn to activities that engage your senses, such as enjoying delicious food, surrounding yourself with soothing music, or immersing yourself in nature's tranquility.

15 Friday

With the Sun in Taurus transiting your second house, your attention turns to financial matters and personal values. This period encourages you to take a pragmatic approach to managing your resources and securing your material well-being. You may feel more motivated to enhance your financial stability and accumulate wealth. It is a time to channel your energy into developing a solid financial foundation and ensuring your values align with your material pursuits.

16 Saturday

The New Moon heralds a fresh beginning, marking the start of a new lunar cycle and offering an opportunity for intention setting, manifestation, and renewal. This celestial event invites you to plant seeds of intention for the future, envision your goals and aspirations, and take proactive steps toward their realization. The New Moon in Gemini enhances communication, curiosity, and adaptability, making it an ideal time for learning, networking, and exploring new ideas.

17 Sunday

At 6:27 AM, Mercury gracefully transitions into Gemini, its home sign, amplifying the influence of communication, intellect, and versatility. In Gemini, Mercury feels right at home, enhancing your mental agility, curiosity, and sociability. This celestial event sparks a desire for lively conversations, intellectual exploration, and the exchange of ideas. You may find yourself more inclined to multitask, adapt to changing circumstances, and embrace variety in your daily life.

MAY

18 Monday

Mars gracefully transitions into Taurus, infusing the atmosphere with a grounded and steadfast energy. In Taurus, Mars encourages you to take a more deliberate and systematic approach to pursuing your desires and goals. This transit invites you to harness the patient and persistent energy of Taurus as you work towards manifesting your ambitions. You may find yourself more determined, focused, and willing to put in the necessary effort to achieve tangible results.

19 Tuesday

At 12:04 AM, Mercury forms a harmonious sextile aspect with Neptune, blending the realms of intellect and intuition in a creative and imaginative union. This aspect enhances your intuition, sensitivity, and spiritual awareness, making it a favorable time for artistic pursuits, spiritual practices, and intuitive insights. You may find that your communication style is more empathetic and compassionate, allowing you to connect with others on a deeper level.

20 Wednesday

The Sun transitions into Gemini, marking a shift in the cosmic energies towards adaptability, communication, and intellectual curiosity. In Gemini, the Sun's influence encourages a more playful and versatile approach to life, inspiring you to explore new ideas, engage in stimulating conversations, and embrace variety and change. This transit heightens your mental agility and encourages you to seek out diverse experiences that stimulate your mind and broaden your horizons.

21 Thursday

With Mercury in Gemini transiting your third house, your communication style and intellectual pursuits become more dynamic and multifaceted. This period encourages you to engage in conversations and learning activities with a focus on curiosity and adaptability. You may find yourself more interested in exploring a wide range of ideas and experiences. This transit is a time to channel your mental energy into developing your communication skills and enhancing your presence.

22 Friday

Venus forms harmonious trine aspects with both the North Node and the South Node, highlighting themes of destiny, growth, and karmic connections in relationships and creative endeavors. These aspects may bring about fated encounters, synchronicities, or opportunities for growth and expansion in matters of love, beauty, and artistic expression. You may feel a sense of alignment with your soul's journey and a deeper connection to your true desires and aspirations.

23 Saturday

At 2:57 AM, the Moon gracefully transitions into Virgo, bringing a shift in focus towards organization, practicality, and attention to detail. In Virgo, the Moon encourages you to analyze, refine, and improve your daily routines, work habits, and health regimens. You may feel a strong desire to be productive, efficient, and organized in your approach to tasks, as well as a heightened sensitivity to orderliness and cleanliness in your surroundings.

24 Sunday

At 9:56 PM, Mars forms both a supportive sextile aspect with the North Node and a harmonious trine aspect with the South Node. These alignments highlight themes of destiny, purpose, and karmic growth in matters related to action, assertion, and personal drive. The sextile to the North Node offers opportunities to align your actions with your soul's evolutionary path, encouraging you to pursue your ambitions with courage, determination, and integrity.

25 Monday

At 10:34 AM, the Moon gracefully transitions into Libra, ushering in a period of harmony, balance, and diplomacy in your emotional landscape. In Libra, the lunar energy seeks fairness, cooperation, and beauty, prompting you to prioritize harmony in your relationships and surroundings. You may feel inclined to seek out peaceful resolutions to conflicts, foster compromise, and cultivate a sense of unity and cooperation with others.

26 Tuesday

At 11:52 AM, the Sun forms a harmonious trine aspect with Pluto, offering an opportunity for empowerment, regeneration, and positive transformation. This aspect brings a sense of depth, intensity, and resilience to your actions and endeavors, allowing you to tap into your inner strength and personal power. You may feel more capable of overcoming obstacles, achieving your goals, and making meaningful changes in your life.

27 Wednesday

The Moon slips into the enigmatic depths of Scorpio, infusing the atmosphere with intense emotions, passion, and a desire for profound transformation. In Scorpio, the lunar energy becomes deeply introspective, seeking to uncover hidden truths, delve into the mysteries of the subconscious, and explore the realms of intimacy and vulnerability. You may find yourself drawn to introspection, seeking to understand the deeper layers of your psyche and emotions.

28 Thursday

When Venus forms a square aspect with Saturn at 11:02 PM, it signifies a challenging alignment between the planet of love, beauty, and harmony and the planet of discipline, limitation, and structure. This aspect may bring about feelings of restriction, inhibition, or delay in matters related to relationships, finances, and creative endeavors. You may encounter obstacles or setbacks in your pursuit of pleasure, affection, or aesthetic fulfillment.

MAY

29 Friday

As the cosmic energies of balance and partnership intertwine, you're encouraged to embrace the principles of equilibrium, fairness, and mutual respect. Today, celestial energies support you in creating harmonious relationships, finding common ground with others, and fostering a sense of unity and cooperation in your endeavors. Trust in the natural cycles of life, and let the energies of balance and beauty guide you toward greater fulfillment and growth.

30 Saturday

The Moon transitions into Sagittarius, infusing the atmosphere with a sense of optimism, adventure, and exploration. In Sagittarius, the lunar energy becomes expansive, enthusiastic, and freedom-loving, encouraging you to seek new experiences, broaden your horizons, and embrace life with a sense of adventure. This lunar transit may inspire you to pursue your passions, embark on spontaneous journeys, or engage in activities that stimulate your mind and spirit.

31 Sunday

At 4:46 AM, the sky illuminates with the brilliance of a Full Moon, marking a significant moment in the lunar cycle when the Sun and Moon oppose each other, casting their light on opposite ends of the zodiac. This Full Moon occurs when the Moon is in Sagittarius, opposing the Sun in Gemini. Full Moons symbolize culmination, completion, and the peak of emotional energy, highlighting areas of your life where you may need to find balance or make adjustments.

JUNE

Mon	Tue	Wed	Thu	Fri	Sat	Sun
1	2	3	4	5	6	7
8	9	10	11	12	13	14
15	16	17	18	19	20	21
22	23	24	25	26	27	28
29	30					

NEW MOON

STRAWBERRY MOON

JUNE

1 Monday

In Capricorn, the lunar energy becomes more reserved, practical, and goal-oriented, encouraging you to take a structured approach to your emotions and objectives. This lunar transit fosters a sense of determination, ambition, and a willingness to work hard to achieve your aspirations. Use this time to set realistic goals, prioritize tasks, and establish a solid foundation for success in both personal and professional endeavors.

2 Tuesday

At 6:48 PM, the Sun forms a harmonious sextile aspect with Saturn, blending the energies of vitality and discipline in a supportive and constructive manner. This aspect brings a sense of stability, responsibility, and endurance, allowing you to focus on long-term goals with confidence and determination. You may find yourself feeling more disciplined, organized, and willing to put in the necessary effort to achieve your ambitions.

3 Wednesday

At 7:39 AM, Mercury forms a harmonious trine aspect with the North Node, indicating a favorable alignment between communication, intellect, and your karmic path. This aspect suggests opportunities for growth, learning, and soulful connections through communication and intellectual pursuits. You may find that your thoughts and ideas align with your higher purpose, leading to insightful conversations and meaningful interactions with others.

4 Thursday

At 9:45 AM, the Moon transitions into Aquarius, infusing the atmosphere with a sense of innovation, independence, and humanitarianism. In Aquarius, the lunar energy becomes progressive, intellectual, and forward-thinking, inspiring you to embrace your individuality and seek out new ways of thinking and being. This lunar transit encourages you to break free from convention, explore unconventional ideas, and connect with like-minded individuals.

5 Friday

With Venus in Cancer transiting your fourth house, your approach to home and family matters becomes more nurturing and emotionally driven. You may find yourself focusing on practical ways to create a harmonious and emotionally supportive domestic environment. This period encourages you to embrace a gentle and protective approach to family life, blending your natural warmth with a desire for emotional connection and security.

6 Saturday

As the Moon ingresses into Pisces, you may find yourself immersed in a world of heightened sensitivity, intuition, and imagination. Your emotional landscape becomes deeply empathetic, and you may feel more attuned to the subtle energies and emotions surrounding you. This lunar transit invites you to embrace your intuitive nature and connect with your innermost feelings. You may feel drawn to creative pursuits, spiritual practices, or moments of quiet introspection.

7 Sunday

With Mars in Taurus transiting your second house, your approach to finances and material possessions becomes more determined and practical. This period encourages you to focus on achieving financial stability and security through careful planning and disciplined actions. You may find yourself more inclined to work hard and invest your resources wisely. This transition is a time to channel your energy into building wealth and ensuring your financial future is secure.

8 Monday

At 6:01 AM, the Moon enters its Last Quarter phase, signifying a pivotal moment in the lunar cycle where the illuminated portion of the Moon diminishes, transitioning from its Full Moon phase towards the New Moon. During this period, you may experience a sense of culmination and reflection as you assess your progress and accomplishments since the beginning of the lunar cycle. It's a time to evaluate what has served its purpose and what needs to be released.

9 Tuesday

At 4:33 AM, the Moon enters your sign, infusing you with a sense of boldness and initiative. This lunar transit ignites your passion and drive, inspiring you to take action and pursue your goals with determination. You may feel a surge of energy and a desire to assert your individuality, making it a favorable time to embark on new beginnings and declare your independence. Embrace the spirit of adventure as you fearlessly navigate through challenges and enjoy opportunities for growth.

10 Wednesday

At 1:37 AM, Mercury squares Saturn, marking a period where communication and mental processes may encounter challenges and restrictions. This aspect suggests a potential clash between the need for expression and the limitations imposed by responsibility or authority figures. You may experience delays and obstacles. It's essential to approach tasks with patience, discipline, and a willingness to confront any challenges with perseverance and determination.

11 Thursday

At 8:27 AM, the Moon ingresses into Taurus, marking a shift in emotional focus and atmosphere. Taurus is an earth sign ruled by Venus, emphasizing stability, comfort, and sensual pleasures. During this lunar transit, emotions tend to become grounded, practical, and focused on tangible comforts and security. There's a greater appreciation for the beauty of nature, indulging in delicious meals, and creating a cozy atmosphere at home.

12 Friday

Uranus square North Node suggests a period of disruptive change and sudden insights that propel you towards your future destiny. This aspect may bring unexpected events or opportunities that challenge your existing path and push you towards new experiences aligned with your soul's evolution. It's a time to embrace innovation, break free from outdated patterns, and embrace the unknown with courage and adaptability.

13 Saturday

At 6:49 AM, Venus gracefully enters Leo, infusing relationships and aesthetic pursuits with warmth, creativity, and a touch of drama. This ingress brings magnetic energy to love and social interactions, inspiring generosity, passion, and a desire for admiration. Under the influence of Leo, Venus encourages self-expression and the pursuit of pleasure, making it an ideal time to indulge in creative endeavors, showcase talents, and bask in the spotlight of romance.

14 Sunday

The New Moon occurring at 10:55 PM marks the beginning of a new lunar cycle, offering a fresh start and a blank canvas for setting intentions and planting seeds for the future. This aspect is a potent time for new beginnings, manifestation, and initiating projects or endeavors. The energy of the New Moon is fertile and receptive, making it an ideal time to clarify your goals, visualize your desires, and take proactive steps toward manifesting your dreams.

15 Monday

At 8:14 AM, the Moon enters its home sign of Cancer, heightening emotional sensitivity and nurturing instincts. This lunar ingress brings a deepening of feelings and a desire for security and comfort. You may find yourself more attuned to your inner world and the needs of those close to you. It's a time for nurturing connections with loved ones, seeking emotional nourishment, and creating a sense of home and belonging.

16 Tuesday

Venus forms a harmonious trine with Neptune, infusing the atmosphere with a sense of enchantment, compassion, and artistic inspiration. This aspect creates a dreamy and romantic ambiance, enhancing our capacity for empathy, creativity, and spiritual connection in matters of love and beauty. It's a time when our hearts open to the subtle nuances of love and appreciation, and we may find ourselves drawn to expressions of beauty, poetry, or music that uplift the soul.

17 Wednesday

At 4:38 PM, Venus opposes Pluto, marking a time of intensity and transformation in your relationships and financial matters. You may experience power struggles or deep emotional insights regarding love, intimacy, and values. This aspect urges you to confront any hidden dynamics or issues within your connections and finances, encouraging honesty and empowerment in these areas. Use this energy to cultivate healthy boundaries and empower yourself in your interactions.

18 Thursday

With Mercury in Cancer transiting your fourth house, your approach to home and family matters becomes more intuitive and nurturing. This period encourages you to engage with family members and plan domestic affairs with a focus on emotional connection and security. You may find yourself more interested in creating a warm and supportive home environment. It is a time to channel your energy into improving your life through empathetic and heartfelt communication.

19 Friday

As the Moon transitions into Virgo at 10:37 AM, a noticeable shift in energy occurs, bringing a focus on practicality, organization, and attention to detail. Virgo is an earth sign associated with precision, efficiency, and a systematic approach to tasks. During this lunar placement, you're likely to feel a strong inclination toward taking care of practical matters and improving the effectiveness of your daily routines.

20 Saturday

With Venus in Leo transiting your fifth house, your approach to creativity, romance, and recreation becomes more confident and expressive. You may find yourself focusing on practical ways to develop your talents and enjoy your leisure activities with a sense of excitement and admiration. This period encourages you to embrace a bold and dynamic approach to creative expression, blending your natural enthusiasm with a desire for recognition and admiration.

21 Sunday

The June Solstice heralds the official start of summer in the Northern Hemisphere and winter in the Southern Hemisphere, occurring at 4:25 AM. This astronomical event marks the longest day of the year for those in the north and the shortest day for those in the south, emphasizing the Earth's tilt towards or away from the Sun. Symbolically, the Solstice represents a shift in energy, highlighting themes of growth, vitality, and abundance, as well as being in harmony with nature's cycles.

22 Monday

The universe is opening doors to new professional opportunities, guiding you toward a path of career advancement and personal growth, where your ambition and collaboration will lead to unprecedented success and satisfaction, enabling you to achieve your goals and realize your dreams. As you seize these opportunities, you will gain valuable skills and insights that will propel you forward, making you a more versatile and dynamic force in your chosen field.

23 Tuesday

The Sun's trine with the North Node highlights a period of alignment with your soul's purpose and destiny. You may feel a sense of clarity, inspiration, and confidence in pursuing your goals and fulfilling your higher calling. This aspect encourages you to embrace new opportunities, expand your horizons, and step into roles or activities that resonate with your authentic self-expression and long-term aspirations. It's a favorable time for personal and spiritual growth.

24 Wednesday

This Moon in Scorpio encourages you to embrace transformation and release what no longer serves your growth. It's a favorable time for psychological insights, uncovering hidden motivations, and addressing any emotional blocks or fears that may be holding you back. Dive deep into your emotions, trust your intuition, and allow yourself to undergo inner healing and regeneration during this lunar phase in Scorpio.

25 Thursday

When Venus forms a trine with Saturn at 8:01 AM, it creates a harmonious and stabilizing influence on matters related to love, relationships, and finances. This aspect signifies a time of commitment, reliability, and groundedness in your interactions and endeavors. You may find that your relationships benefit from increased stability, loyalty, and a sense of mutual support. It's a favorable period for making plans, solidifying commitments, and building lasting foundations.

26 Friday

The Sagittarius Moon encourages you to embrace a sense of wanderlust, both physically and mentally. Whether you're exploring new places, delving into different cultures, or expanding your knowledge through education and self-discovery, this lunar phase supports your quest for personal and spiritual expansion. Stay open-minded, embrace diversity, and allow the Sagittarius Moon to ignite your curiosity and passion for life's adventures.

27 Saturday

The Sun in Cancer in the fourth house enhances your ability to communicate and connect with your family members. You're likely to be more open to discussing family matters and finding creative solutions to any challenges that arise. This influence can bring about a period of positive change in your home life as you embrace new approaches. By staying communicative, you can strengthen your family bonds and create a supportive and nurturing home environment.

28 Sunday

When Mars forms a sextile with Jupiter at 12:50 AM, it creates a dynamic and promising aspect that brings a surge of energy, enthusiasm, and optimism. This planetary alignment combines the assertive and action-oriented nature of Mars with the expansive and optimistic influence of Jupiter. As a result, you may feel driven to pursue your goals with confidence, take calculated risks, and seize opportunities for growth and success.

JULY

Mon	Tue	Wed	Thu	Fri	Sat	Sun
		1	2	3	4	5
6	7	8	9	10	11	12
13	14	15	16	17	18	19
20	21	22	23	24	25	26
27	28	29	30	31		

New Moon

BUCK MOON

_____

_____

_____

_____

_____

_____

_____

_____

_____

_____

_____

_____

_____

_____

_____

_____

_____

_____

_____

30 Monday

Overall, this day's astrological influences encourage you to embrace structure and responsibility while navigating Mercury retrograde with caution and mindfulness. Use the Full Moon energy to let go of what no longer aligns with your goals and aspirations, allowing space for new beginnings and growth. Focus on practicality, patience, and self-reflection as you navigate the energies of the Moon in Capricorn, Mercury retrograde, and the Full Moon.

31 Tuesday

The astrological events today bring a mix of challenging aspects and expansive energies. At 1:31 AM, Mars forms square aspects with both the North Node and the South Node simultaneously. This alignment can create tension and conflicts related to your path forward and past influences. You may feel a pull between taking assertive action towards your future goals (North Node) and addressing unresolved issues or patterns from the past (South Node).

1 Wednesday

The Aquarius Moon fosters a sense of community and inclusivity, making it an excellent time for social gatherings, virtual meetings, or connecting with friends and acquaintances who inspire you. Embrace the spirit of cooperation, diversity, and forward-thinking as you navigate the energies of the Aquarius Moon. Use this time to contribute positively to collective efforts and expand your horizons intellectually and socially.

2 Thursday

Celestial energies are enhancing your intuition, providing you with insights and guidance that help you navigate life's challenges with wisdom and clarity. This period of heightened intuition will allow you to make better decisions and avoid potential pitfalls, leading to more tremendous success and happiness. Trusting your inner voice empowers you to take decisive actions and pursue opportunities that align with your true purpose, fostering a sense of inner peace and confidence.

3 Friday

With Mars in Gemini transiting your third house, your communication style and intellectual pursuits become more energetic and versatile. This period encourages you to engage in lively discussions, share your ideas, and absorb new information with enthusiasm. You may find yourself more willing to take initiative in learning and networking. This transit is a time to channel your energy into developing your communication skills and expanding your intellectual horizons.

4 Saturday

The Mars sextile Neptune aspect enhances your intuition, creative vision, and ability to manifest your dreams and aspirations. It's a favorable time for pursuing artistic projects, spiritual practices, or endeavors that require a blend of passion and intuition. Trust your instincts, follow your heart, and channel the harmonious energy of Mars and Neptune to bring about positive transformations in your life and align your actions with your higher purpose.

5 Sunday

Today's astrological influence of Mars trine Pluto is a powerful catalyst for personal transformation, empowerment, and achievement. It encourages you to embrace challenges as opportunities for growth, tap into your inner warrior spirit, and take bold steps toward realizing your dreams and aspirations. With determination, resilience, and a willingness to confront inner depths, you can harness the transformative energy of Mars and Pluto to create positive change.

6 Monday

When the Sun forms a square aspect with Saturn at 6:47 AM, a sense of tension and responsibility may color the early hours of the day. This aspect highlights potential challenges related to authority, structure, and limitations. You may feel a need to confront obstacles or face reality in a particular area of your life. While this aspect can bring about a sense of discipline and determination, it's essential to approach tasks with patience, resilience, and a willingness to learn from setbacks.

7 Tuesday

Later in the afternoon, at 3:30 PM, the Moon reaches its Last Quarter phase, marking a pivotal point in the lunar cycle. This phase invites you to release, let go, and reflect on the progress made since the New Moon. It's a time to review the intentions set, evaluate what is working or not working in your life, and make adjustments as needed. The Last Quarter Moon encourages closure, completion, and preparation for the upcoming New Moon cycle.

8 Wednesday

When the Moon transitions into Taurus at 4:30 PM, a sense of stability, comfort, and groundedness settles in, bringing a shift towards practicality, security, and a focus on the material world. The Taurus Moon encourages you to prioritize your physical well-being, enjoy sensory pleasures, and cultivate a sense of abundance and security in your surroundings. This lunar ingress promotes a sense of calmness, patience, and appreciation for life's simple pleasures.

9 Thursday

When Venus transitions into Virgo at 1:25 PM, a shift towards practicality, attention to detail, and a focus on refinement takes place in matters of love, relationships, and aesthetics. The Venus in Virgo influence encourages you to approach love and beauty with a discerning eye, emphasizing qualities such as practicality, organization, and reliability. It's a favorable time for paying attention to small gestures and showing appreciation through acts of service.

10 Friday

When Venus opposes the North Node at 6 AM, a dynamic tension arises between your desires for love, beauty, and harmony (Venus) and your karmic path and destiny (North Node). This aspect may bring up challenges or conflicts in relationships, highlighting areas where growth, balance, and alignment with your life's purpose are needed. It's a time to reassess your values, priorities, and approach to partnerships, seeking harmony and authenticity.

11 Saturday

With the Sun in Cancer transiting your fourth house, your focus is on home, family, and emotional foundations. This period encourages you to create a dynamic and communicative environment within your domestic sphere. You may feel more inclined to connect with family members, engage in discussions, and make changes to your living situation. Use this time to enhance your home life and build stronger emotional bonds.

12 Sunday

Under the influence of the Cancer Moon, you may feel more attuned to your inner world, intuitive insights, and the needs of those closest to you. It is a favorable time for bonding with family, expressing empathy and compassion, and engaging in activities that foster emotional connections and a sense of belonging. Use this period to nurture yourself and others, cultivate a sense of emotional security, and strengthen bonds with loved ones.

13 Monday

The Venus-Uranus square challenges traditional norms and invites you to embrace individuality, authenticity, and non-conformity in your relationships and aesthetic preferences. You may feel inclined to break free from restrictions, explore new experiences, or pursue unconventional forms of expression in matters of love, beauty, and creativity. Use this aspect as an opportunity to express your unique style and desires, embracing the freedom to be yourself.

14 Tuesday

When the New Moon occurs at 5:44 AM, a decisive lunar phase begins, symbolizing fresh starts and opportunities for growth and manifestation. It is a potent time for setting intentions, planting seeds of intention for the future, and initiating projects or endeavors that align with your goals and aspirations. Embrace the energy of the New Moon to focus on what you want to create and manifest in your life, setting the stage for positive transformations.

15 Wednesday

Overall, the Uranus sextile Neptune aspect offers a gateway to higher consciousness, innovative ideas, and spiritual growth. Use this time to connect with your inner wisdom, explore new realms of creativity and inspiration, and allow the universe to guide you toward fulfilling your dreams and aspirations with a sense of flow and synchronicity. Embrace the magic and mystery of life as you navigate this harmonious alignment between Uranus and Neptune.

16 Thursday

Overall, the Moon's ingress into Virgo invites you to embrace practicality, organization, and attention to detail. Take advantage of this time to streamline your routines, focus on tasks that require precision, and make practical improvements that contribute to your overall well-being and success. Use the Virgo Moon's energy to bring order and efficiency to your life, creating a foundation for productivity and personal fulfillment.

17 Friday

During today's energies, you may experience flashes of inspiration, creative solutions to problems, and a heightened ability to grasp complex concepts quickly. It's an excellent time for brainstorming, experimenting with new ideas, and embracing unconventional approaches to communication and learning. Use this dynamic energy to explore innovative solutions, engage in stimulating conversations, and express your ideas with confidence and enthusiasm.

18 Saturday

The harmonious aspect between Uranus and Pluto encourages you to explore innovative ideas, pursue creative endeavors, and make bold changes that align with your vision for the future. It's a favorable time for exploring new technologies, unconventional solutions, and progressive approaches to problem-solving. Embrace your inner revolutionary spirit and embrace opportunities to make a positive impact in your life and the world around you.

19 Sunday

When the Moon transitions into Libra at 12:57 AM, harmonious and diplomatic energy begins to influence the atmosphere, promoting balance, harmony, and a focus on relationships and cooperation. The Libra Moon encourages you to seek harmony in your interactions, prioritize fairness and compromise, and cultivate a sense of peace and collaboration in your environment. This lunar ingress invites you to embrace diplomacy and tactfulness, fostering positive connections.

20 Monday

The Jupiter-Neptune trine encourages you to embrace your dreams, tap into your intuition, and envision possibilities beyond the ordinary. It's a favorable time for artistic endeavors, spiritual practices, and connecting with your higher purpose and aspirations. Use this cosmic alignment to explore your imagination, seek higher wisdom, and align your actions with your ideals and values. Allow yourself to trust in the guidance of your intuition and embrace the journey of self-discovery.

21 Tuesday

At 7:10 AM, Jupiter forms a harmonious sextile aspect with Uranus, creating an atmosphere of innovation, expansion, and unexpected opportunities. This planetary alignment encourages you to embrace change, explore new possibilities, and welcome unconventional ideas and approaches. Use this cosmic synergy to think outside the box, pursue exciting ventures, and embrace the spirit of adventure and experimentation.

22 Wednesday

Overall, the Sun's shift into Leo invites you to embrace your inner fire, express yourself boldly, and live life with passion and enthusiasm. Use this cosmic energy to ignite your creativity, inspire others with your unique gifts, and embody the qualities of leadership, self-expression, and authenticity. Trust in your ability to shine brightly, make a positive impact, and embrace the adventure of being true to yourself in all aspects of your life.

23 Thursday

When Mercury stations direct at 6:58 PM, a shift in communication, clarity, and decision-making begins to unfold, marking the end of its retrograde period. This celestial event brings a sense of forward movement, allowing for smoother communication, clearer thinking, and greater ease in making plans and decisions. Embrace this shift as an opportunity to resolve misunderstandings, move past delays, and focus on moving forward with confidence and purpose.

24 Friday

When Mercury forms a sextile aspect with Venus at 12:08 PM, harmonious and pleasant energy infuses the day, enhancing communication, social interactions, and creative expression. This planetary alignment brings a blend of intellect and charm, making it an excellent time for heartfelt conversations, negotiations, and artistic endeavors. The Mercury-Venus sextile encourages you to express your thoughts and feelings with grace, tact, and diplomacy.

25 Saturday

When Neptune forms a sextile aspect with Pluto, a potent and transformative energy infuses the cosmic landscape, offering opportunities for deep spiritual insights, inner growth, and profound transformation. This harmonious alignment between the mystical Neptune and the powerful Pluto signifies a time of spiritual awakening, emotional healing, and empowerment on a soul level. The Neptune-Pluto sextile invites you to delve into the depths of your subconscious.

26 Sunday

At 3:29 PM, Saturn turns retrograde, marking a period of introspection, reassessment, and karmic lessons. During Saturn's retrograde phase, you're encouraged to review your commitments, responsibilities, and areas where you may need to exercise greater discipline and maturity. Use this time to reflect on your long-term goals, address any limitations or obstacles, and strengthen your foundations for future success.

27 Monday

When the Sun opposes Pluto at 2:55 AM, a powerful and transformative energy permeates the cosmic landscape, bringing potential challenges, power struggles, and opportunities for profound inner transformation. This aspect may bring intense encounters, revelations of hidden truths, and a need to confront power dynamics in various areas of life. Embrace this transit as an opportunity to release control, let go of old patterns, and empower yourself through self-awareness.

28 Tuesday

When the Moon transitions into Aquarius at 9:46 PM, a shift towards intellectual exploration, innovation, and humanitarian ideals influences the cosmic atmosphere. The Aquarius Moon encourages you to embrace your uniqueness, think outside the box, and connect with like-minded individuals who share your vision for positive change. This lunar ingress invites you to break free from societal norms, embrace your individuality, and advocate for causes that resonate.

29 Wednesday

When Venus squares Mars at 3:09 AM, a dynamic and potentially tense energy unfolds, highlighting themes of passion, desire, and relationship dynamics. This aspect may bring conflicts or challenges in matters of love, intimacy, or creative expression. It encourages you to find a balance between assertiveness and diplomacy in your interactions and to address any underlying tensions with patience and understanding.

30 Thursday

In the face of today's cosmic rays, trust in your inner wisdom and resilience to navigate through any challenges that come your way. Embrace the lessons of the past as stepping stones towards a brighter future, and remain steadfast in your commitment to your personal and spiritual evolution. Allow yourself to surrender to the flow of life, knowing that each experience, whether joyful or challenging, is an integral part of your journey toward wholeness and self-realization.

AUGUST

Mon	Tue	Wed	Thu	Fri	Sat	Sun
					1	2
3	4	5	6	7	8	9
10	11	12	13	14	15	16
17	18	19	20	21	22	23
24	25	26	27	28	29	30
31						

NEW MOON

_____

_____

_____

_____

_____

_____

_____

_____

_____

_____

_____

_____

_____

_____

_____

_____

_____

_____

_____

_____

_____

STURGEON MOON

31 Friday

When the Moon transitions into Pisces at 8:14 AM, a dreamy, imaginative, and sensitive energy permeates the cosmic atmosphere, inviting you to delve into the realms of intuition, creativity, and emotional depth. The Pisces Moon encourages compassion, empathy, and a deep connection with your inner world and the unseen aspects of life. Allow yourself to surrender to the flow of emotions and tap into the intuitive wisdom that Pisces brings.

1 Saturday

With Venus in Virgo transiting your sixth house, your approach to work, health, and daily routines becomes more organized and detail-oriented. You may find yourself focusing on ways to improve your productivity and well-being with precision and practicality. This period encourages you to embrace a thoughtful and meticulous approach to your daily tasks, blending your natural energy with a desire for order and improvement.

2 Sunday

When the Moon transitions into Aries at 4:36 PM, a surge of dynamic, energetic, and assertive energy fills the cosmic atmosphere, igniting a sense of enthusiasm, passion, and courage. The Aries Moon encourages you to embrace boldness, take initiative, and pursue your goals with determination and vigor. This lunar ingress marks a time of increased motivation and drive, empowering you to overcome challenges and make bold strides toward your aspirations.

3 Monday

With the Sun in Leo transiting your fifth house, your focus is on creativity, romance, and self-expression. This period encourages you to embrace your artistic talents and engage in activities that bring you joy and excitement. You may feel more inclined to seek out romantic connections and enjoy the pleasures of life. Use this time to express your emotions through creative outlets and pursue your passions with enthusiasm.

4 Tuesday

When the Moon transitions into Taurus at 10:35 PM, a sense of stability, comfort, and grounded energy permeates the cosmic atmosphere, inviting you to slow down, savor the present moment, and connect with your senses. The Taurus Moon encourages you to focus on practical matters, material comforts, and nurturing your well-being. This lunar ingress brings a soothing and nurturing energy, inviting you to find serenity and contentment in the simple joys of life.

5 Wednesday

During the Last Quarter Moon, you may feel a sense of culmination and closure regarding projects, goals, or emotional cycles that have been unfolding since the New Moon. It's a time to assess your achievements, acknowledge lessons learned, and release any attachments or obstacles that may be hindering your growth and progress. Use this phase to reflect on your intentions set during the New Moon and make any necessary adjustments or revisions.

6 Thursday

Under the influence of Venus in Libra, you may feel a stronger desire for harmony, beauty, and social connections. This transit encourages you to seek balance in your relationships, appreciate aesthetics and artistic expressions, and engage in activities that promote peace, love, and mutual respect. Embrace the Venusian energy to nurture meaningful connections and cultivate a sense of unity and partnership in your personal and professional interactions.

7 Friday

Under the influence of the Gemini Moon, you may feel more mentally alert, friendly, and eager to explore diverse perspectives and interests. This lunar ingress invites you to embrace curiosity, engage in learning experiences, and connect with others through meaningful communication and interactions. Embrace the opportunity to share your thoughts and ideas, fostering engaging conversations and expanding your understanding of the world around you.

8 Saturday

The Sun in Leo in the fifth house enhances your ability to express yourself with confidence and flair. You're likely to be more attuned to your creative side and more willing to take risks in pursuing your passions. This influence can bring about a period of artistic growth and romantic opportunities as you embrace your inner radiance. By focusing on activities that bring you joy and emotional fulfillment, you can create a more vibrant and satisfying life.

9 Sunday

Today's astrological influences highlight the importance of nurturing emotional well-being, connecting with loved ones, and expressing yourself authentically. Embrace the nurturing energy of the Cancer Moon to foster emotional healing and create a sense of security and comfort. Embrace the expressive and creative power of Mercury in Leo to share your ideas and talents with passion and confidence. Connect with others as you navigate the energies of the day.

10 Monday

Mars forms a supportive sextile aspect with the South Node and a harmonious trine aspect with the North Node simultaneously at 11:38 PM, signaling a time of karmic realignment and forward momentum. The Mars sextile South Node aspect encourages you to release old patterns, habits, or conflicts that may be hindering your progress. Embrace this opportunity to let go of what no longer serves your growth and evolution, paving the way for new beginnings and positive changes.

11 Tuesday

Venus forms a trine aspect with Uranus at 11:45 PM, bringing unexpected and exciting opportunities for love, creativity, and personal freedom. This harmonious aspect between Venus and Uranus encourages you to embrace spontaneity, explore new experiences, and welcome unconventional connections or expressions of love and beauty. Be open to surprises and be willing to step outside your comfort zone to embrace the magic of unexpected blessings.

12 Wednesday

Mercury forms a harmonious sextile aspect with Uranus, bringing a surge of innovative thinking, mental clarity, and intellectual breakthroughs. This aspect encourages you to think outside the box, embrace unconventional ideas, and communicate with originality and spontaneity. Use this time to brainstorm, problem-solve creatively, and share your unique insights and perspectives with others. Embrace the freedom to express yourself authentically.

13 Thursday

The Moon's ingress into Virgo brings a focus on practicality, organization, and attention to detail. This transit encourages you to analyze, plan, and approach tasks with efficiency and precision. Use this time to attend to responsibilities, prioritize your to-do list, and create a sense of order in your daily routines and environment. Embrace the Virgoan energy to streamline your activities, improve productivity, and find satisfaction in accomplishing tasks with accuracy.

14 Friday

With Mercury in Leo transiting your fifth house, your approach to creativity, romance, and recreation becomes more confident and expressive. This period encourages you to pursue your passions and desires with a lively and bold mindset. You may find yourself more interested in engaging in creative projects that allow you to showcase your talents. This is a time to channel your mental energy into creating joyful and meaningful experiences through engaging efforts.

15 Saturday

At 7:23 AM, Mercury forms a powerful conjunction with Jupiter, amplifying intellectual abilities, expanding perspectives, and fostering optimism and enthusiasm in communication and thought processes. This aspect encourages broad-minded thinking, positive exchanges, and a focus on growth, learning, and exploring new possibilities. Embrace this conjunction to seek knowledge, engage in meaningful discussions, and expand your mental horizons.

16 Sunday

With Venus in Libra transiting your seventh house, your relationships and partnerships take on a new level of harmony and balance. This period encourages you to focus on creating equality in your interactions. Your charm and diplomatic nature are highlighted, making it easier to form and maintain harmonious connections. You may find yourself more attuned to the needs of your partner and willing to compromise for the sake of peace and mutual understanding.

17 Monday

Your ruling planet, Mars, forms a challenging square aspect with Neptune, creating a potential for confusion, low energy, and unclear motivations. This aspect may bring about challenges in asserting yourself effectively or taking decisive action. It's essential to stay grounded, clarify intentions, and avoid getting swept away by unrealistic expectations or deceptive influences. Use this time to practice mindfulness, prioritize self-care, and avoid making impulsive decisions.

18 Tuesday

The cosmos is sending waves of harmonious energy, urging you to find balance and equilibrium in all aspects of your life. This period is perfect for reassessing priorities, aligning your actions with your values, and fostering a sense of inner peace. As you harmonize your personal and professional spheres, you'll experience a newfound sense of stability and well-being that supports your overall growth and happiness.

19 Wednesday

The Moon's First Quarter marks a pivotal moment in the lunar cycle, signaling a time of action, initiative, and decision-making. This lunar phase encourages you to take proactive steps toward your goals, address any challenges or obstacles, and make adjustments as needed to stay on track with your intentions and aspirations. Embrace the energy of the First Quarter Moon to assess your progress, identify areas of improvement, and take decisive action to move forward.

20 Thursday

The Moon's ingress into Sagittarius at 4:30 AM brings a shift in energy, highlighting themes of exploration, adventure, and philosophical expansion. This lunar transit encourages you to embrace spontaneity, seek new experiences, and broaden your horizons both mentally and physically. Use this time to engage in activities that inspire curiosity, stimulate learning, and encourage a sense of freedom and optimism.

21 Friday

When Venus opposes Saturn at 8:42 AM, a sense of tension and restriction may arise in matters related to love, relationships, and finances. This aspect can bring about challenges in expressing affection, experiencing joy, or achieving harmony in partnerships. It's essential to be patient, realistic, and responsible in your interactions and commitments during this time. Embrace the lessons that the Venus-Saturn opposition brings, such as the need for boundaries or commitment.

22 Saturday

The Moon's ingress into Capricorn at 4:59 PM brings a shift in emotional focus towards responsibility, ambition, and practicality. This lunar transit encourages you to take a disciplined approach to your emotions, prioritize long-term goals, and work towards achieving stability and success in various areas of life. Use this time to set realistic expectations, organize your tasks efficiently, and demonstrate resilience in the face of challenges.

23 Sunday

Mars in Cancer in the fourth house enhances your ability to manage family affairs with emotional insight and determination. You may feel the drive to achieve domestic goals through protective efforts. This transit is a time to approach your home life with a caring and emotionally grounded mindset, allowing your intuitive strength to create a secure and supportive environment. Embrace this opportunity to strengthen your family bonds, creating a home that is nurturing.

24 Monday

The stars are aligning to promote a period of strategic planning and goal setting, offering you the clarity and foresight needed to map out your future. It is a time to envision your dreams, set achievable milestones, and develop a roadmap for success. The cosmic energy empowers you to take decisive actions, harness your potential, and make significant strides toward realizing your aspirations. The universe supports your journey of self-empowerment, helping you to shine.

25 Tuesday

At 6:10 AM, Mercury opposes the North Node and conjuncts the South Node simultaneously, highlighting themes of communication, learning, and karmic evolution. The Mercury-North Node opposition may bring challenges or insights related to your life path, communication style, or areas where growth is needed. It's essential to be open to new perspectives, engage in meaningful conversations, and adapt your thinking to align with your soul's journey.

26 Wednesday

With the Sun in Virgo transiting your sixth house, your focus is on work, health, and daily routines. This period encourages you to establish efficient and practical habits that promote your well-being and productivity. You may feel more inclined to organize your workspace and prioritize tasks that enhance your professional life. Use this time to review and improve your health routines, ensuring that they support your overall vitality. A meticulous approach helps you maintain balance.

27 Thursday

Embrace the Sun-Mercury conjunction to enhance your communication skills, convey your thoughts effectively, and seek clarity in your interactions. Utilize the Pisces Moon's energy to connect with your inner wisdom, explore your dreams and fantasies, and cultivate compassion and empathy towards yourself and others. Trust in your intuition and allow yourself to flow with the emotional currents of this Piscean lunar phase for deeper insights and emotional healing.

28 Friday

The Full Moon at 12:19 AM marks a culmination of energies, illuminating areas of your life where you may experience heightened emotions, awareness, and revelations. This lunar phase encourages you to release what no longer serves you, embrace closure, and celebrate achievements or completions. Use this time to reflect on your goals, intentions, and progress and consider any necessary adjustments or transformations moving forward.

29 Saturday

The Moon's ingress into Aries marks a shift towards assertiveness, independence, and action-oriented energy. This lunar transit encourages you to embrace your inner drive, take initiative, and pursue your goals with enthusiasm and determination. Use this time to channel your passion, cultivate courage, and embark on beginnings or projects that ignite your spirit. Embrace the dynamic energy of the Aries Moon to assert your needs and express yourself authentically.

30 Sunday

Celestial influences are fostering a time of deep emotional connection and intimacy, encouraging you to open your heart and share your innermost feelings with those you love. It is an ideal moment to strengthen your relationships, build trust, and deepen bonds through heartfelt conversations and shared experiences. The universe supports your efforts to create a foundation of love and understanding that enriches your life and brings joy to your connections.

SEPTEMBER

Mon	Tue	Wed	Thu	Fri	Sat	Sun
	1	2	3	4	5	6
7	8	9	10	11	12	13
14	15	16	17	18	19	20
21	22	23	24	25	26	27
28	29	30				

New Moon

CORN/HARVEST MOON

_____

_____

_____

_____

_____

_____

_____

_____

_____

_____

_____

_____

_____

_____

_____

_____

_____

_____

31 Monday

Embrace the positive synergy of Jupiter trine Saturn to cultivate a sense of purpose, establish solid foundations, and pursue opportunities that align with your values and long-term vision. Use this time to invest in your future, expand your knowledge or skills, and build a sense of stability and security in critical areas of your life. Trust in your abilities, stay focused on your goals, and leverage this supportive cosmic energy to manifest positive outcomes and personal fulfillment.

1 Tuesday

Mars forms a challenging square aspect with Saturn, highlighting potential frustrations, obstacles, and limitations in your actions and endeavors. This aspect may require patience, perseverance, and strategic planning to overcome hurdles and achieve your goals. Avoid impulsive actions, stay focused on long-term objectives, and use this energy to cultivate discipline and determination. Trust in your ability to overcome challenges and remain committed to your path.

2 Wednesday

Mercury in Virgo in the sixth house enhances your ability to manage your work and health with precision and practicality. You may feel more driven to achieve professional and personal goals through meticulous and well-organized efforts. Embrace this opportunity to transform your daily habits, creating a lifestyle that is both productive and fulfilling. Your analytical skills can lead to increased efficiency and effectiveness in your work environment.

3 Thursday

The Moon's ingress into Gemini at 7:47 AM brings a shift towards curiosity, communication, and versatility. This lunar transit encourages mental agility, social interactions, and a desire for new experiences. Use this time to engage in stimulating conversations, learn something new, and adapt quickly to changing circumstances. Embrace the playful and curious energy of the Gemini Moon to explore diverse interests and connect with others intellectually.

4 Friday

The Moon's Last Quarter marks a phase of reflection, assessment, and closure as the lunar cycle nears its completion. This lunar aspect encourages you to review your progress, release what no longer serves your growth, and prepare for new beginnings. Use this time to let go of old patterns, complete unfinished tasks, and set intentions for what you wish to manifest in the future. Embrace the transformative energy of the Last Quarter Moon to release old habits.

5 Saturday

As the Moon enters Cancer, you may feel a heightened sense of empathy and a desire to connect with your innermost feelings. Use this reflective energy to explore your emotional landscape, process any unresolved emotions, and strengthen your emotional bonds with those you care about. Trust in the wisdom of your intuition and allow yourself to express vulnerability and authenticity during this sensitive lunar transit.

6 Sunday

The cosmos is enhancing your ability to manifest your desires, encouraging you to focus on your intentions and visualize your goals with clarity and conviction. This period is perfect for practicing manifestation techniques, such as creating vision boards or affirmations, to attract what you want into your life. The celestial energies support your manifestation journey, guiding you toward opportunities and resources that align with your desires.

7 Monday

The Moon's ingress into Leo at 12:49 PM invites you to step into the limelight and embrace your creative flair. This lunar transit encourages you to express yourself boldly, take risks, and seek opportunities to showcase your talents and skills. Use this time to pursue activities that ignite your passion, engage your creativity, and bring joy and fulfillment to your life. Embrace the confidence and charisma of the Leo Moon to make a positive impact and leave your mark on the world.

8 Tuesday

The Sun in Virgo in the sixth house enhances your ability to manage your daily responsibilities with precision and care. You're likely to be more attentive to your health and work routines, making it an excellent time to implement positive changes. This influence can bring about a period of personal growth as you focus on creating a balanced and healthy lifestyle. By staying organized and proactive in your daily tasks, you can make a more productive and fulfilling life.

9 Wednesday

Embrace the analytical energy of the Moon's ingress into Virgo. This lunar transit encourages you to focus on practical matters, improve your organizational skills, and attend to your physical and mental health with diligence. Allow yourself to be thorough in your approach, make thoughtful choices, and strive for a sense of balance and efficiency in all aspects of your life. Use the Virgo Moon's energy to bring order and clarity to your thoughts, actions, and surroundings.

10 Thursday

The New Moon at 11:28 PM marks a potent moment for new beginnings, intentions, and planting seeds of growth and manifestation. This lunar phase encourages you to set clear intentions, visualize your desires, and take proactive steps toward your goals. Use the energy of the New Moon to initiate projects, start fresh chapters, and align your actions with your long-term vision for success and fulfillment. Trust in the natural cycles of growth and transformation.

11 Friday

Embrace the harmonious and diplomatic energy of the Moon's ingress into Libra at 7:52 PM. This lunar transit encourages you to seek balance, promote peace, and cultivate a sense of unity in your relationships and social interactions. Use the Libra Moon's influence to enhance communication, find common ground, and foster mutual respect and understanding. Trust in the power of cooperation and collaboration as you navigate this harmonious and graceful lunar phase.

12 Saturday

Mercury's opposition to Neptune at 12:37 PM introduces a contrasting energy of confusion, illusion, and potential misunderstandings. This aspect may bring challenges in communication, leading to unclear messages or deceptive information. It's essential to be mindful of potential miscommunications, misunderstandings, or unrealistic expectations during this time. Take extra care to verify facts and clarify intentions.

13 Sunday

The trine between Mercury and Uranus enhances your ability to grasp complex concepts quickly, adapt to changing circumstances, and express your ideas in unique and exciting ways. This aspect favors brainstorming sessions, technological advancements, and out-of-the-box thinking. Embrace the electric energy of Mercury trine Uranus to break free from mental limitations, embrace your eccentricities, and share your vision for the future.

14 Monday

The Moon's ingress into Scorpio at 2:44 AM intensifies emotional depth, introspection, and a focus on transformation and regeneration. This lunar transit encourages you to delve into the hidden realms of your psyche, confront deep-seated emotions, and embrace the power of renewal and healing. Use this time to engage in reflective practices, such as meditation or journaling, to explore your inner world and gain insights into your emotional landscape.

15 Tuesday

The Venus square Pluto aspect at 2:33 PM brings intensity, passion, and potential challenges in relationships and financial matters. This aspect may highlight power struggles, control issues, or deep-seated emotional dynamics that need to be addressed and transformed. It's essential to navigate this influence with honesty, integrity, and a willingness to confront underlying issues for healing and growth. Use this period to delve deep into your emotions and release any toxic patterns.

16 Wednesday

Overall, today's astrological influence of the Moon in Sagittarius invites you to embark on a journey of self-discovery, growth, and adventure. Embrace the spirit of exploration and curiosity as you navigate new territories and expand your understanding of life's possibilities. Trust in your ability to navigate unknown paths with courage and optimism, knowing that each step forward brings valuable insights and opportunities for personal development.

17 Thursday

With Venus in Scorpio transiting your eighth house, your approach to intimacy and shared resources becomes profoundly intense and transformative. This period encourages you to delve into the deeper aspects of your intimate relationships and financial partnerships, seeking to uncover hidden truths and foster mutual trust. You may find yourself more willing to explore emotional and economic complexities, leading to greater understanding and growth.

18 Friday

At 6 AM, the challenging aspect of Mercury, as opposed to Saturn, creates a celestial tension that may bring about communication blocks, delays, or a sense of restriction in mental clarity. It's a time when responsibilities, limitations, or critical thinking may hinder the flow of ideas or conversations. Patience and perseverance are essential during this aspect, as they encourage you to find practical solutions and work through any obstacles with diligence and focus.

19 Saturday

When the Moon gracefully transitions into Capricorn at 12:55 AM, the cosmic energy takes on a grounded and pragmatic tone, encouraging you to embody qualities of discipline, responsibility, and ambition as you navigate the unfolding chapters of your journey. This lunar shift invites you to connect with your inner sense of structure and organization, empowering you to approach tasks with a methodical mindset and a focus on long-term success.

20 Sunday

As you move through the day, remain vigilant yet open-hearted, embracing each moment with a spirit of curiosity and humility. Recognize that within the subtle whispers of the universe lie hidden treasures of insight and revelation, guiding you along your path of growth and discovery. Allow yourself to be guided by the currents of cosmic energy, finding solace and guidance in the sanctuary of your inner knowing amidst the ebb and flow of today's celestial influence.

21 Monday

As the Aquarius Moon and the Mercury-Jupiter sextile align in the celestial symphony, you're encouraged to embrace your unique perspectives, communicate with clarity and conviction, and collaborate with others to bring about positive change. This aspect is a time to harness the power of innovation, expand your mental horizons, and contribute to collective endeavors that uplift and inspire. Trust in the cosmic flow of inspiration and growth, and let your unique light shine.

22 Tuesday

Under the influence of the Libra Sun, you may feel drawn to harmonious interactions, seeking peace and understanding in your connections with others. This solar ingress encourages you to approach conflicts with grace and diplomacy, prioritize cooperation over competition, and strive for mutual benefit and compromise in your partnerships. Let the Libra Sun inspire you to cultivate empathy, understanding, and a spirit of collaboration in all your relationships.

23 Wednesday

Overall, today's Moon's ingress into Pisces signifies a time of heightened sensitivity, spiritual awakening, and emotional depth. Embrace the subtle energies of this lunar phase, listen to the whispers of your soul, and allow yourself to be guided by the mystical currents of the Piscean realm. Trust in the power of intuition, empathy, and imagination to guide you on your journey of self-discovery, spiritual growth, and compassionate living.

24 Thursday

Mercury in Libra in the seventh house sharpens your ability to negotiate and collaborate effectively with partners. You may feel more driven to achieve relationship goals through organized and balanced efforts. Embrace this opportunity to refine your partnership dynamics, creating connections that are both stable and harmonious. Your diplomatic approach will help resolve conflicts and improve cooperation, fostering a supportive atmosphere.

25 Friday

When the Sun opposes Neptune at 9:36 PM, the cosmic energies create a dance of contrast between clarity and illusion, reality and dreams. This astrological aspect invites you to navigate the fine line between fantasy and truth, encouraging discernment and a deeper understanding of the unseen forces at play. It's a time to reflect on your beliefs, ideals, and perceptions, allowing space for introspection and exploration of the mystical realms that Neptune symbolizes.

26 Saturday

When the Sun forms a harmonious trine with Pluto at 1:34 AM, the cosmic energies align to empower transformation, renewal, and personal growth. This aspect encourages you to tap into your inner strength, resilience, and ability to regenerate aspects of your life that are ready for change. It's a time to embrace empowerment, embrace transformation, and harness your inner resources to overcome challenges and achieve your goals.

27 Sunday

Overall, Mars's ingress into Leo heralds a time of bold action, creative expression, and empowered self-confidence. Embrace your inner fire, unleash your passions, and let your unique light shine as you navigate the exciting opportunities and challenges that lie ahead. Trust in your abilities, follow your heart's desires, and boldly pursue your dreams with courage and conviction. Allow Mars in Leo to inspire you to lead with passion, creativity, and authenticity.

OCTOBER

Mon	Tue	Wed	Thu	Fri	Sat	Sun
			1	2	3	4
5	6	7	8	9	10	11
12	13	14	15	16	17	18
19	20	21	22	23	24	25
26	27	28	29	30	31	

NEW MOON

HUNTERS MOON

28 Monday

The Sun forms a harmonious trine with Uranus, sparking innovation, spontaneity, and a sense of liberation. This astrological aspect encourages you to embrace change, explore new ideas, and break free from old patterns or restrictions. It's a time to think outside the box, embrace your individuality, and welcome unexpected opportunities for growth and expansion. Use this dynamic energy to shake things up, try new approaches, and invite positive changes into your life.

29 Tuesday

When Mercury forms a harmonious trine with the North Node, the cosmic energies align to facilitate communication, learning, and connections that are aligned with your soul's purpose. This aspect encourages you to engage in meaningful conversations, share knowledge, and seek information that supports your evolution. It's a favorable time for learning new skills, making meaningful connections, and aligning your thoughts and ideas with your higher path.

30 Wednesday

Overall, the combination of Mercury in Scorpio and the Gemini Moon invites you to engage in meaningful conversations, explore new ideas, and expand your mental horizons. Embrace the opportunities for introspection, intellectual growth, and transformative insights that arise during this time. Trust in your ability to navigate complexity, communicate effectively, and uncover hidden truths that can lead to personal and intellectual evolution.

1 Thursday

The Sun in Libra in the seventh house enhances your ability to engage with others in a diplomatic and considerate manner. You're likely to be more focused on creating harmonious relationships, making it an excellent time to address any issues that may have caused friction. This influence can bring about a period of mutual growth and a profound understanding as you work towards shared goals. By prioritizing fairness and balance in your interactions, you can cultivate peace.

2 Friday

When Mercury forms a challenging square with Mars at 5:13 AM, the cosmic energies may bring about potential conflicts in communication, impulsive decisions, or a tendency towards argumentative behavior. It's essential to practice patience, think before speaking or acting, and avoid unnecessary confrontations. Use this aspect as an opportunity to channel your mental energy into productive tasks, exercise caution in discussions, and avoid rushing into hasty decisions.

3 Saturday

At 3:14 AM, Venus, the planet of love and relationships, begins its retrograde journey, prompting a period of introspection and reevaluation in matters of the heart. This cosmic shift invites you to review your values, reassess your relationships, and reflect on what brings true fulfillment and harmony into your life. It's a time to address unresolved issues, heal past wounds, and gain clarity on your emotional needs and desires.

4 Sunday

Overall, today's astrological influences encourage a balance between responsibility and self-expression. Embrace the lessons of the Sun-Saturn opposition by staying committed to your goals and duties while also allowing the Leo Moon to inspire confidence, creativity, and a joyful approach to life. Find ways to express yourself authentically, overcome challenges with determination, and celebrate your achievements along the way.

5 Monday

With the Sun in Libra transiting your seventh house, your focus shifts to relationships, partnerships, and one-on-one interactions. This period encourages you to bring balance, fairness, and harmony into your personal and professional relationships. You may feel more inclined to compromise and work towards mutual understanding in your partnerships. Use this time to nurture and strengthen your connections with others, fostering cooperation and collaboration.

6 Tuesday

Overall, today's astrological influences encourage harmonious communication, practicality, and attention to detail. Take advantage of the Mercury-Venus conjunction to express love, appreciation, and understanding in your interactions. Use the Virgo Moon's energy to enhance productivity, organization, and self-care. Embrace a balanced approach that combines heartfelt connections with practical actions, leading to greater harmony, efficiency, and well-being in your life.

7 Wednesday

The Mars sextile Uranus aspect supports collaborative efforts, group activities, and teamwork that incorporate innovative solutions and forward-thinking strategies. It's a time to collaborate with like-minded individuals, share your unique ideas, and contribute to collective initiatives that promote progress and positive change. Explore synergies with others, foster creative collaborations, and harness the power of collective intelligence to achieve meaningful outcomes.

8 Thursday

The universe is inspiring your literary talents, encouraging you to put pen to paper and explore the world of creative writing. Whether it's starting a journal, writing poetry, or crafting a novel, this is a time for expressive and imaginative endeavors. The celestial energies are providing a fertile ground for your creativity to flourish, helping you articulate your thoughts and stories with clarity and passion. Embrace this opportunity to share your unique voice with the world.

OCTOBER

9 Friday

The Libra Moon's energy highlights aesthetics, beauty, and the appreciation of art and culture. It's a favorable time for indulging in activities that enhance your sense of beauty, such as visiting art galleries, listening to soothing music, or spending time in aesthetically pleasing surroundings. This lunar phase encourages you to surround yourself with beauty, find inspiration in artistic expressions, and cultivate a sense of harmony in your personal space.

10 Saturday

The New Moon's energy amplifies the potential for new beginnings, fresh perspectives, and a sense of renewal. Take advantage of this cosmic opportunity to set intentions, visualize your dreams, and take proactive steps toward manifesting your desires. Use rituals or practices that resonate with you, such as meditation, journaling, or visualization, to align your energy with your intentions and create a clear path forward.

11 Sunday

When the Moon transitions into Scorpio at 11:21 AM, an intense energy permeates the atmosphere, urging you to delve into the mysteries of life and explore the depths of your emotions. The Scorpio Moon's influence brings a sense of passion and transformation, encouraging you to embrace the power of introspection and inner growth. This lunar shift invites you to tune into your intuition and trust the wisdom that arises from your innermost being.

12 Monday

An enterprising area brings a chance to rebrand your image. It grows your talents and harnesses creative thinking to set your sights higher. You raise the bar and learn an area that increases your knowledge and heightens your abilities. It gives you a chance to build a site that brings new possibilities into your environment. As you move forward towards advancing to the next level, you reshape goals and revolutionize the potential possible in your world.

13 Tuesday

When the Moon transitions into Sagittarius at 8:59 PM, a sense of adventure and optimism fills the air, inspiring you to explore new horizons and embrace exciting opportunities. The Sagittarius Moon's influence brings a spirit of curiosity and freedom, encouraging you to approach life with a sense of wonder and openness to new experiences. This lunar shift invites you to embrace spontaneity and welcome the unexpected with enthusiasm and optimism.

14 Wednesday

Mercury in Scorpio in the eighth house enhances your ability to handle complex issues related to shared resources and intimacy with intensity and insight. You may feel more driven to achieve transformation and growth through focused and well-thought-out efforts. Embrace this opportunity to refine your approach to shared responsibilities, creating a balanced and equitable environment. Your problem-solving skills can lead to increased trust and understanding.

15 Thursday

When the Sun forms a sextile with Jupiter at 4:21 AM, harmonious and expansive energy infuses the cosmos, bringing opportunities for growth, optimism, and abundance. This aspect combines the vitality of the Sun with the vast and philosophical nature of Jupiter, creating a favorable atmosphere for personal and professional advancement. This celestial alignment encourages you to believe in your abilities and take bold steps toward your aspirations.

16 Friday

When Mars forms a trine with Saturn at 4:32 AM, harmonious and disciplined energy permeates the cosmos, providing a stable foundation for pursuing your goals with determination and persistence. This aspect combines Mars' drive and initiative with Saturn's structure and discipline, empowering you to take practical and strategic actions toward long-term success. This celestial alignment encourages you to work diligently and follow through with commitments.

17 Saturday

With Mars in Leo transiting your fifth house, your approach to creativity, romance, and recreation becomes more passionate and dramatic. This period encourages you to pursue your passions and desires with confidence and flair, focusing on activities that bring joy and excitement. You may find yourself more willing to take risks and express your creativity in bold and innovative ways. This is a time to channel your energy into creating joyful and inspiring experiences.

18 Sunday

Later in the day, at 9:40 PM, the Moon transitions into Aquarius, ushering in a period of innovation, collaboration, and humanitarian ideals. The Aquarius Moon's influence inspires you to think outside the box, connect with like-minded individuals, and contribute to collective endeavors. Use this lunar transit to embrace your uniqueness, explore new ideas, and engage in meaningful interactions with others, fostering a sense of unity and shared purpose.

19 Monday

You gain a glimpse of glittering possibilities and soon thrive in a busy and active environment. An area that has been on the backburner for a while gets the shift forward. It helps you sort out and organize the aspects of your life that have become disruptive. Streamlining and juggling demands draw the essence of efficiency to progress your life forward effectively. A powerful influence flows into your world, setting the stage for an enterprising chapter of growth.

20 Tuesday

Overall, the Venus-Pluto square brings a potent energy that calls for honesty, introspection, and empowerment in relationships and financial matters. Approach challenges with empathy and understanding, prioritize open communication and healthy boundaries, and use this period for personal and relational growth. By confronting underlying issues and embracing transformation, you can emerge more substantial and more aligned with your authentic self.

21 Wednesday

In the morning, at 8:35 AM, the Moon transitions into Pisces, infusing the atmosphere with sensitivity, intuition, and a deep connection to the subconscious mind. The Pisces Moon's influence encourages empathy, creativity, and spiritual exploration, making it an ideal time for introspection, artistic pursuits, and connecting with your innermost emotions. Embrace this intuitive energy to dive deep into your feelings and gain insights into your emotional landscape.

22 Thursday

Fortune shines upon your life as you transition to a positive chapter that brings sunny skies overhead. Changes surrounding your social life ensure you are busy. New opportunities to mingle emerge, which helps you develop forward momentum. It opens the door to a social environment that enlivens and nurtures your spirit. It lets you spend more time with friends and share thoughts, leading to collaboration ahead.

23 Friday

The combination of the Sun's ingress into Scorpio, the Moon's ingress into Aries, and the Sun's conjunction with Venus creates a dynamic and transformative energy that encourages self-discovery, assertiveness, and emotional depth. Trust in your intuition, embrace the passion and vitality of the moment, and allow yourself to be guided by your inner fire and desire for authentic expression. This period offers opportunities for personal growth and passionate endeavors.

24 Saturday

As Mercury turns retrograde at 3:13 AM, it signals a time for introspection, reflection, and revisiting past decisions and communication patterns. This retrograde period invites you to slow down, review your plans and projects, and address any unresolved issues or miscommunications that may have arisen in recent weeks. Use this cosmic shift as an opportunity to gain clarity, refine your strategies, and realign your thoughts and actions with your long-term goals.

25 Sunday

As Venus gracefully enters Libra at 5:04 AM, it brings with it an aura of harmony, balance, and a renewed focus on relationships and aesthetic pleasures. This celestial shift encourages you to seek beauty in all aspects of life, foster harmonious connections, and prioritize fairness and diplomacy in your interactions. Embrace this time as an opportunity to create a more balanced and serene environment, both within yourself and in your relationships with others.

26 Monday

As the Full Moon graces the night sky at 12:12 AM, its luminous presence signifies a time of culmination, heightened emotions, and the potential for profound insights. This lunar phase invites you to bask in its radiant energy, reflect on your journey thus far, and celebrate the progress you've made on your path. Embrace the Full Moon's illumination as a beacon of clarity, guiding you to release what no longer serves your highest good and embrace new beginnings.

27 Tuesday

At 9:02 PM, the Moon gracefully transitions into Gemini, ushering in a period of curiosity, versatility, and intellectual stimulation. This lunar ingress invites you to embrace a more adaptable and communicative approach to life, explore new ideas, and engage in meaningful conversations that broaden your perspective. With the Moon in Gemini, your mind may be more agile and receptive to diverse perspectives and information, making it a favorable time for learning.

28 Wednesday

With Saturn in Aries transiting your first house, your focus is on self-discipline, personal responsibility, and identity. This period encourages you to take a serious and structured approach to your personal growth and self-expression. You may feel a strong urge to redefine your goals and establish clear boundaries. Use this time to build a solid foundation for your future, hone your leadership skills, and assert your independence.

29 Thursday

The Cancer Moon's influence encourages you to prioritize self-care, honor your feelings, and create a harmonious balance between your personal and professional life. Use this time to recharge your emotional batteries, engage in activities that bring you comfort and joy, and nurture your emotional well-being. Embrace moments of quiet reflection and introspection to deepen your connection with yourself and your innermost desires.

NOVEMBER

Mon	Tue	Wed	Thu	Fri	Sat	Sun
						1
2	3	4	5	6	7	8
9	10	11	12	13	14	15
16	17	18	19	20	21	22
23	24	25	26	27	28	29
30						

New Moon

BEAVER MOON

30 Friday

The harmonious aspects between Venus and the lunar nodes at 6:13 PM bring a blend of destiny and opportunity in relationships and creative expressions. Embrace the supportive influences that foster growth, connection, and alignment with your soul's journey while consciously releasing any past attachments or behaviors that no longer serve your highest good. Trust in the natural rhythms of life, follow your heart's guidance, and cultivate harmony and fulfillment.

31 Saturday

With the Sun in Scorpio transiting your eighth house, your focus is on transformation, shared resources, and deep emotional connections. This period encourages you to explore the depths of your emotional and financial life, seeking ways to create stability and security. You may feel more inclined to delve into the mysteries of life and uncover hidden truths. Use this time to engage in transformative experiences that foster growth and healing.

1 Sunday

As the Moon enters its last Quarter phase, reflect on your aspirations, honor your progress, and release any fears or doubts that may hinder your growth. Trust in your inner wisdom, stay aligned with your purpose, and prepare to step into a new chapter with clarity, resilience, and a renewed sense of purpose. Be ready to embrace the exciting opportunities that lie ahead and manifest your dreams with determination and optimism.

2 Monday

The universe is aligning to bring clarity and purpose to your career path, urging you to align your professional endeavors with your true passions and talents. This period is perfect for setting ambitious goals, pursuing opportunities for growth and advancement, and making meaningful contributions in your chosen field. The celestial energies support your career journey, guiding you toward success and fulfillment in your professional pursuits.

3 Tuesday

At 3:28 AM, the Moon gracefully transitions into Virgo, ushering in a period of practicality, organization, and a meticulous focus on details. This lunar ingress encourages you to approach tasks with efficiency, prioritize your responsibilities, and strive for excellence in your daily routines and endeavors, fostering a sense of order and productivity in your life. Enjoy the earthy energy of Virgo as you engage in practical activities and create structured plans.

4 Wednesday

Venus forms a harmonious sextile with Jupiter, creating a celestial atmosphere filled with optimism, abundance, and a sense of expansion in relationships and creative pursuits. This aspect encourages you to embrace opportunities for personal growth, broaden your horizons, and infuse your interactions with positivity and joy, fostering harmonious connections and a sense of fulfillment. Use this alignment to explore and connect with others authentically.

5 Thursday

When the Moon transitions into Libra, a harmonious and balanced energy permeates the atmosphere, emphasizing the importance of harmony, cooperation, and diplomacy in your interactions and relationships. The Libra Moon encourages you to seek balance, fairness, and mutual understanding in your connections with others, fostering a sense of peace in your environment. This celestial shift invites you to approach your relationships with grace and empathy.

6 Friday

With Jupiter in Leo transiting your fifth house, your focus is on creativity, romance, and self-expression. This period encourages you to explore your creative passions and engage in activities that bring joy and fulfillment. You may feel more inclined to pursue romantic interests and express your love openly. Use this time to embrace your artistic talents and enjoy the pleasures of life. An adventurous approach to creativity and romance will help you attract positive experiences.

7 Saturday

Under the influence of the Scorpio Moon, you may feel a heightened sense of passion, intuition, and a desire for profound connections. This lunar ingress encourages you to delve beneath the surface, uncover hidden truths, and embrace vulnerability as a path to personal growth and empowerment. Use this time to connect with your innermost desires, tap into your intuition, and trust the wisdom that arises from your depths.

8 Sunday

The Sun in Scorpio in the eighth house enhances your ability to handle intense and transformative experiences with resilience and insight. You're likely to be more focused on creating stability in your emotional and financial life. This influence can bring about a period of profound relational growth as you work through challenges and seek deeper connections. By embracing a balanced approach to transformation, you can achieve emotional and financial security.

9 Monday

Overall, the New Moon at 2:03 AM signifies a potent moment for setting intentions, embracing new beginnings, and aligning with your highest aspirations. Embrace the energy of potential and possibility, trust in your inner guidance, and take inspired action toward creating the life you desire. Allow yourself to dream big, believe in your dreams, and take steps towards manifesting a fulfilling and purposeful life filled with abundance and joy.

10 Tuesday

When Venus forms a sextile aspect with Mars at 1:45 AM, harmonious and dynamic energy flows between the realms of love, passion, and creativity. This celestial alignment creates a favorable atmosphere for harmonizing desires, expressing affection, and taking decisive action in matters of the heart and creative endeavors. Embrace this harmonious aspect to strengthen relationships, enhance romantic connections, and channel your creative energies with enthusiasm.

11 Wednesday

Amidst the bustling energy of social gatherings, where laughter fills the air and friendships are forged, there's a sense of camaraderie that binds you together like threads in a tapestry. It's a time when your heart resonates with the joy of connection, when shared experiences become cherished memories, and when the warmth of companionship lights up even the darkest of nights. So, let yourself embrace the vibrancy of social interactions.

12 Thursday

When Jupiter opposes the North Node and simultaneously conjuncts the South Node, a complex dynamic emerges in the cosmic energies, emphasizing themes of growth, destiny, and karmic lessons. This planetary alignment may bring about a sense of tension between expansion and past patterns, urging you to examine where you're headed versus where you've come from. It's a time to reflect on your ambitions, beliefs, and the lessons you've learned along your life path.

13 Friday

When Mercury turns direct, a shift in communication and clarity occurs, marking the end of a period of introspection and reassessment. This planetary event brings a sense of forward movement, mental clarity, and a reduction in communication glitches or misunderstandings. Use this time to express yourself more confidently, make decisions based on clear thinking, and move forward with plans and projects that may have been on hold during Mercury retrograde.

14 Saturday

The Mars opposition to the North Node, in conjunction with the South Node, prompts you to examine how your actions and desires align with your soul's evolutionary path. It's a time to confront any tendencies towards impulsiveness, aggression, or ego-driven pursuits that may be pulling you away from your true purpose. Embrace this opportunity to let go of old patterns, align with your higher self, and take conscious action that serves your long-term goals and aspirations.

15 Sunday

When the Moon ingresses into Aquarius at 4:24 AM, it ushers in a shift in emotional focus towards a more detached and intellectual perspective. You may find yourself drawn to unconventional ideas, progressive thinking, and a desire for freedom and individuality in your emotional expression. This transit encourages you to explore new ways of connecting with others, emphasizing cooperation, community involvement, and humanitarian concerns.

16 Monday

When Mars aligns with Jupiter in conjunction, it signifies a potent fusion of energy and expansion. Mars, the planet of action, drive, and assertiveness, joining forces with Jupiter, the planet of growth, optimism, and abundance, creates a dynamic and ambitious atmosphere. This conjunction encourages boldness, enthusiasm, and a strong desire to achieve significant goals. It's a celestial invitation to step into your power and embrace opportunities with confidence.

17 Tuesday

The Sun squares both the North Node and the South Node, creating a tense aspect that emphasizes karmic lessons and life path adjustments. The Sun square North Node challenges you to step out of your comfort zone and align with your soul's purpose, while the Sun square South Node urges you to release old patterns and beliefs that no longer serve your growth. This astrological alignment invites you to confront past conditioning and embrace transformative change.

18 Wednesday

Today's square aspect challenges you to find a middle ground between ambition and practicality. While Jupiter encourages growth, opportunity, and abundance, the square from the Sun may highlight areas where you need to exercise restraint or reevaluate your goals, prompting a period of reflection and adjustment. Use this energy to refine your strategies, prioritize effectively, and focus on sustainable progress, harnessing the tension to fuel constructive changes.

19 Thursday

When the Sun squares Mars at 12:49 PM, it ignites a dynamic and potentially confrontational energy, urging you to be mindful of impulsivity and assertiveness. This aspect can bring about tension, impatience, and a strong desire to assert oneself, emphasizing the need for patience and strategic planning in navigating challenges. It's crucial to harness this fiery energy for constructive purposes and avoid unnecessary conflicts by choosing your battles wisely.

20 Friday

When the Moon ingresses into Aries, it heralds a shift towards assertiveness, action, and initiative. Aries, a fiery and energetic sign ruled by Mars, encourages boldness, courage, and a willingness to take on challenges head-on, prompting you to embrace a proactive approach to achieving your ambitions. This lunar transit ignites independence and self-confidence, urging you to pursue your goals with enthusiasm and determination while staying true to your authentic self.

21 Saturday

Celestial forces ignite a spark of inspiration within your soul, fueling your creativity and empowering you to express yourself authentically. This is a time for embracing your unique gifts and talents and allowing your creative spirit to soar. The universe supports your creative endeavors, providing opportunities for artistic expression and innovation. Embrace this period of creative inspiration, knowing that your creativity has the power to inspire and uplift others.

22 Sunday

When the Sun ingresses into Sagittarius at 2:26 AM, it ushers in a period of exploration, optimism, and expansion. Sagittarius, ruled by Jupiter, encourages a broad perspective, a thirst for knowledge, and a sense of adventure. This solar transit invites you to embrace new experiences, seek higher truths, and cultivate a spirit of optimism and enthusiasm. It's a time to broaden your horizons, set lofty goals, and approach life with a renewed sense of curiosity and wonder.

23 Monday

When Venus forms a trine aspect with the North Node at 7:33 AM, it signifies a harmonious alignment between love, relationships, and your karmic path. This aspect brings opportunities for positive connections, soulmate encounters, and fulfilling partnerships that support your growth and evolution. It's a time to embrace love, harmony, and collaboration in your interactions, fostering meaningful and supportive relationships that align with your life's purpose.

24 Tuesday

At 9:54 AM, the Full Moon occurs, illuminating the sky with its radiant energy. The Full Moon represents culmination, completion, and heightened emotions. It's a time of clarity, revelations, and manifestations, where intentions set during the New Moon come to fruition. Use this decisive lunar phase to celebrate achievements, release what no longer serves you, and align with your goals and desires. Reflect on your journey and express gratitude for your accomplishments.

25 Wednesday

The Sun forming a sextile with Pluto brings a harmonious alignment between power and transformation. This aspect encourages you to delve deep into your inner strengths, make positive changes, and embrace opportunities for growth and empowerment. It's a favorable time for self-discovery, healing, and stepping into your authenticity with confidence. Use this alignment to tap into your resilience and ability to overcome obstacles, harnessing transformative energies.

26 Thursday

The Moon in Cancer heightens your empathy, compassion, and desire for emotional closeness. It's a favorable time for self-care activities, spending time with family, and expressing your feelings openly. Allow yourself to tune into your intuition and honor your emotions during this lunar phase, as they provide valuable insights and guidance. Use this period to strengthen emotional bonds, offer support to loved ones, and create a nurturing atmosphere in your home.

27 Friday

With the Sun in Sagittarius illuminating your ninth house, your focus shifts to higher learning, travel, and philosophical exploration. This period encourages you to embrace your adventurous spirit and seek out new experiences that expand your horizons. You may feel a strong desire to embark on a journey of self-discovery, whether through travel to distant lands or through the pursuit of knowledge and wisdom. Use this time to broaden your intellectual horizons.

28 Saturday

Venus forms a sextile aspect with Jupiter, creating a harmonious alignment between love, abundance, and optimism. This aspect fosters a positive outlook on relationships, finances, and personal values. It's a time for expanding your social circle, enjoying pleasurable experiences, and attracting abundance and opportunities through a positive mindset. Use this auspicious alignment to cultivate gratitude, nurture connections, and seek out experiences that enrich.

29 Sunday

When Uranus forms a trine aspect with Pluto, it signifies a harmonious alignment between revolutionary change and profound transformation. This aspect brings about a powerful synergy between innovation and regeneration, allowing for significant breakthroughs and positive shifts in various areas of life. It's a time for embracing change, releasing old patterns, and stepping into a new phase of growth and empowerment. Use this cosmic energy to catalyze positive shifts in your life.

December

Mon	Tue	Wed	Thu	Fri	Sat	Sun
	1	2	3	4	5	6
7	8	9	10	11	12	13
14	15	16	17	18	19	20
21	22	23	24	25	26	27
28	29	30	31			

NEW MOON

COLD MOON

30 Monday

The combination of the Sun trine Saturn and the Moon ingress into Virgo creates a balanced and productive energy. It's a time for disciplined action, practicality, and responsible decision-making. Embrace a structured approach to your goals, focus on tasks that require concentration and effort, and prioritize tasks that contribute to your long-term success. Use this supportive cosmic influence to build a solid foundation for your endeavors and make progress toward your ambitions.

1 Tuesday

At 1:09 AM, the last quarter moon phase marks a pivotal moment for you in the lunar cycle, urging you to reflect on the progress made since the recent New Moon. It's a time for assessment and adjustment as you navigate the challenges and opportunities that have arisen throughout the month. This phase encourages you to let go of what no longer serves you and to focus your energy on completing unfinished tasks or releasing habits that hinder your growth.

2 Wednesday

At 3:04 PM, the Moon transitions into Libra, infusing your emotional landscape with a desire for harmony, balance, and social connection. Libra, ruled by Venus, seeks beauty and diplomacy in all interactions, encouraging you to approach relationships and situations with a sense of grace and fairness. During this lunar ingress, you may find yourself more attuned to the needs and perspectives of others, striving to find common ground and foster cooperation.

3 Thursday

With Mars in Virgo transiting your sixth house, your approach to work, health, and daily routines becomes more disciplined and organized. This period encourages you to focus on achieving professional and personal well-being through meticulous and methodical efforts. You may find yourself more willing to take on tasks that require careful planning and attention to detail. This is a time to channel your energy into creating a balanced and efficient daily life.

4 Friday

At 2:02 AM, you may feel the tension as Mercury squares Jupiter, challenging your thoughts and communication. This aspect can lead to exaggerated ideas or promises, so it's crucial to maintain a balanced perspective and avoid overcommitting or taking on too much. Be mindful of potential misunderstandings or conflicts arising from differences in opinions or beliefs, and strive to communicate with clarity and honesty to navigate this aspect effectively.

5 Saturday

In the ninth house, the Sun in Sagittarius inspires you to embrace the spirit of adventure and exploration in your quest for knowledge and understanding. You may feel a sense of excitement and enthusiasm as you pursue higher learning, travel to exotic destinations, or engage in philosophical debates with others. This influence encourages you to trust in your intuition and follow your curiosity wherever it may lead you.

6 Sunday

Mercury transitions into Sagittarius, infusing your thoughts and communication with expansive and adventurous energy. In Sagittarius, Mercury seeks truth, wisdom, and philosophical understanding, encouraging you to broaden your perspectives and explore new horizons through open-minded inquiry and exploration. This transit inspires a thirst for knowledge and a desire to engage in meaningful conversations that expand your understanding of the world.

7 Monday

You may experience a sense of stability and focus as Mercury forms a harmonious trine with Saturn. This alignment encourages disciplined thinking and communication, making it an excellent time for structured planning, organization, and strategic thinking. You'll likely find it easier to concentrate on tasks that require attention to detail and long-term vision. This aspect also supports constructive conversations and negotiations.

8 Tuesday

At 5:29 AM, you may encounter unexpected twists and turns as Mercury opposes Uranus, sparking sudden insights and breakthroughs in your thinking and communication. This aspect can bring about a sense of restlessness and excitement, urging you to embrace change and innovation. Be prepared for surprises or disruptions to your plans, as Uranus encourages you to think outside the box and consider unconventional solutions to any challenges that arise.

9 Wednesday

At 8:40 AM, brace yourself for potential conflicts or tensions in communication as Mercury squares Mars. This aspect can lead to impulsive reactions, sharp words, or disagreements, so it's crucial to think before speaking and avoid jumping to conclusions. Channel this dynamic energy constructively by engaging in physical activity or finding creative outlets for any pent-up frustration. Use diplomacy and patience to navigate any challenges that arise.

10 Thursday

Saturn's direct motion serves as a cosmic reminder of the importance of patience, perseverance, and resilience. While Saturn's influence can sometimes feel restrictive or challenging, its ultimate aim is to help you build strength, resilience, and self-mastery. As Saturn moves forward, you are encouraged to embrace the responsibilities and commitments that come with your chosen path, knowing that through dedication and hard work, you can overcome any obstacles.

11 Friday

At 8:25 AM, you'll likely experience a harmonious alignment between Mercury and Saturn, marking a moment of stability and clarity in your mental landscape. This aspect fosters a sense of practicality and focus, making it an excellent time for planning, organizing, and tackling tasks that require careful attention to detail. With Mercury's quick wit and Saturn's disciplined approach working in tandem, you'll find that your thoughts are grounded and your communication is clear.

12 Saturday

A harmonious alignment unfolds between Venus and Mars as they form a sextile aspect, igniting passion and creativity in your interpersonal relationships and pursuits. This celestial dance encourages harmonious interactions, fostering a sense of attraction, balance, and mutual understanding between you and others. Whether in romantic endeavors or creative collaborations, this alignment enhances your ability to express your desires with grace and charm.

13 Sunday

With Jupiter in Leo transiting your fifth house, your focus is on creativity, romance, and self-expression. This period encourages you to explore your passions and engage in activities that bring joy. You feel more inclined to pursue romantic interests and express your love openly. Use this time to embrace your artistic talents and enjoy the pleasures of life. An adventurous and enthusiastic approach to creativity and romance will help you attract positive experiences.

14 Monday

At 3:59 AM, a significant astrological event occurs as the Sun forms both a sextile with the North Node and a trine with the South Node. This rare alignment highlights a balance between your past and future, offering opportunities for growth and evolution while also providing a chance to integrate lessons from the past. The North Node represents your karmic path and future direction, while the South Node signifies past experiences and patterns to release.

15 Tuesday

You may find yourself drawn to activities that involve travel, learning, or connecting with people from different cultures and backgrounds. Use this time to embark on new adventures, expand your knowledge and understanding of the world, and embrace the opportunities for growth and discovery that come your way. Allow yourself to be inspired by the boundless possibilities that lie ahead, and trust in the wisdom of your intuition to guide you on your journey.

16 Wednesday

Mercury in Sagittarius in the ninth house enhances your ability to pursue higher learning and philosophical exploration with optimism and insight. You may feel more driven to achieve academic and spiritual goals through focused and well-thought-out efforts. Embrace this opportunity to refine your intellectual pursuits, creating connections that are both enlightening and practical. Your analytical approach can help you delve deeper into complex subjects.

17 Thursday

With the Moon in Aries and the First Quarter phase in full swing, you're encouraged to tap into your inner strength and resilience as you navigate the opportunities and challenges that arise. Trust in your instincts and embrace the spirit of adventure as you chart your course forward. This is a time for bold action, self-discovery, and embracing the thrill of the unknown. Seize the moment and harness Aries' dynamic energy to propel yourself towards your goals.

18 Friday

A harmonious celestial alignment occurs as the Sun forms a trine with Jupiter, amplifying optimism, abundance, and expansion. This auspicious aspect brings a sense of opportunity and good fortune, encouraging you to embrace a positive outlook and seize the possibilities that surround you. Jupiter, the planet of growth and wisdom, expands the energy of the Sun, illuminating your path with clarity and inspiration. Under this influence, you may feel a surge of confidence.

19 Saturday

At 3:29 PM, the Moon gracefully transitions into Taurus, ushering in a period of stability, comfort, and sensual pleasure. Taurus, ruled by Venus, invites you to indulge in life's simple pleasures and luxuriate in the beauty of the physical world. Under this lunar influence, you may find yourself drawn to activities that engage your senses, such as enjoying delicious food, surrounding yourself with beauty, or immersing yourself in nature's abundance.

20 Sunday

With Mercury sextile the North Node, your thoughts and communication are aligned with your higher path and spiritual evolution. This aspect supports clear and insightful communication, making it an ideal time for expressing your intentions, sharing ideas, and connecting with others on a soul level. Embrace the opportunity to align your words with your soul's purpose, and trust that your interactions are guided by divine wisdom and intuition.

21 Monday

The December Solstice marks a significant astronomical event, signaling the beginning of winter in the Northern Hemisphere and summer in the Southern Hemisphere. This celestial phenomenon heralds the shortest day and longest night of the year, inviting you to turn inward and embrace the reflective energy of the season. It's a time for reflection, renewal, and setting intentions for the cycle ahead as you honor the rhythm of nature and the changing of the seasons.

22 Tuesday

In the enchanting tapestry of Christmas week, every passing day unfolds like a cherished storybook, brimming with moments of wonder, warmth, and shared joy that dance in harmony with the twinkling lights and festive melodies. From the hushed anticipation of Christmas Eve to the jubilant celebrations of Christmas Day and the serene days that follow, each hour is a precious gift, offering opportunities for connection, reflection, and the creation of lasting memories.

23 Wednesday

As the day dawns, the cosmic dance between the radiant Sun and mystical Neptune brings forth a moment of introspection and spiritual attunement. Under this celestial alignment, you may be encouraged to tread with caution, for the veils between the seen and unseen realms may blur, casting illusions upon your path. It is a time to delve deep into the depths of your subconscious, confronting any shadows or illusions that may cloud your vision.

24 Thursday

The magic of Christmas infuses your surroundings with beauty and wonder as celestial energies inspire you to embrace the enchanting spirit of the season. It is a time for marveling at the twinkling lights, festive decorations, and sparkling ornaments that adorn your home and neighborhood. The universe supports your sense of awe, guiding you toward opportunities for creativity, inspiration, and artistic expression.

25 Friday

As Mercury ingresses into Capricorn at 1:25 PM, you may feel a shift in your communication style and mental focus. This transit encourages a pragmatic and disciplined approach to thinking and decision-making. You may find yourself more inclined to think in practical terms and prioritize long-term goals over short-term gratification. Use this time to organize your thoughts, set realistic plans, and communicate with authority and clarity.

26 Saturday

As Mercury gracefully moves through the celestial expanse, it encounters the elusive influence of Neptune at 2:46 PM. This alignment, known as Mercury square Neptune, may cast a subtle veil of confusion or illusion over your thoughts and perceptions. In this delicate dance between the planet of communication and the nebulous depths of Neptune, be mindful of the potential for misunderstandings and misinformation.

27 Sunday

As the moon gracefully transitions into the meticulous realm of Virgo at 5:13 PM, you are invited to embrace the energies of practicality and discernment. Virgo's influence encourages you to pay attention to the details of your daily life and to cultivate a sense of order and efficiency in your actions. Allow yourself to approach tasks with a methodical mindset, focusing on the small steps that lead to more remarkable accomplishments. Trust in the process of refinement.

28 Monday

Saturn in Aries in the first house enhances your ability to confront challenges head-on and develop a strong sense of self. You are likely to experience significant personal growth as you take on more responsibilities and set firm goals for yourself. This influence can bring about a period of rigorous self-examination and transformation, where you redefine your identity and purpose. By embracing a proactive approach, you can lay the groundwork for long-term achievements.

29 Tuesday

As Venus forms challenging squares with both the North Node and the South Node at 4:42 PM, you may feel a tug-of-war between the past and the future in matters of love, relationships, and values. These aspects urge you to confront any lingering karmic patterns or unresolved issues from the past that may be hindering your growth. Embrace this opportunity to release old attachments and step into alignment with your soul's evolutionary path.

30 Wednesday

Mercury forms a challenging square with Saturn at 6:54 PM, highlighting potential obstacles or limitations in communication and mental clarity. This aspect may bring delays, restrictions, or feelings of frustration in your ability to express yourself or convey your ideas effectively. Take a patient and disciplined approach to any mental challenges that arise, dear one, trusting that they offer opportunities for growth and refinement in your communication skills.

31 Thursday

Mercury forms a supportive trine with Mars at 6:30 PM, further amplifying your mental understanding and communication skills. This aspect enhances your ability to articulate your thoughts and ideas with precision and conviction. Seize this opportunity to express yourself boldly and assertively, trusting in the power of your words to inspire and motivate others. Harness the synergistic energy of Mercury and Mars to tackle intellectual challenges with confidence.

2026 List of Astrological Events

The time zone is America Eastern Time, EST. The GMT offset is -5:00.

January

Thursday 1st
Sun sextile North Node 5:22 AM
Sun trine South Node at 5:22 AM
Mercury Square Neptune 8:33 AM
Mercury ingress Capricorn 4:12 PM
Friday 2nd
Venus sextile North Node 2:27 AM
Venus trine South Node 2:27 AM
Moon ingress Cancer 8:09 AM
Saturday 3rd
Full Moon 5:04 AM
Sunday 4th
Moon ingress Leo 8:43 AM
Tuesday 6th
Moon ingress Virgo 11:56 AM
Thursday 8th
Mercury sextile North Node 7:07 AM
Mercury trine South Node 7:07 AM
Moon ingress Libra 7:06 PM
Friday 9th
Venus opposed Jupiter 12:34 PM
Saturday 10th
Sun opposed Jupiter 3:42 AM
Mars opposed Jupiter at 9:25 AM
Moon last Quarter at 10:49 AM
Sunday 11th
Moon ingress Scorpio 5:55 AM
Tuesday 13th
Moon ingress Sagittarius 6:34 PM
Wednesday 14th
Mercury opposed Jupiter at 3:17 AM
Thursday 15th
Venus sextile Saturn 1:18 AM
Venus trine Uranus 10:22 AM
Friday 16th
Moon ingress Capricorn 6:47 AM
Saturday 17th
Venus sextile Neptune 3:33 AM
Sun sextile Saturn 5:41 AM
Venus ingress Aquarius 7:45 AM
Sun trine Uranus 11:58 AM
Sunday 18th
New Moon 2:53 PM
Moon ingress Aquarius 5:18 PM
Mercury sextile Saturn 11:09 PM
Monday 19th
Mercury trine Uranus 12:37 AM
Sun sextile Neptune 4:54 PM
Sun ingress Aquarius 8:47 PM
Tuesday 20th
Saturn sextile Uranus 12:18 AM
Mars trine Uranus 12:56 AM
Mars sextile Saturn 1:01 AM
Mercury sextile Neptune 9:34 AM
Mercury ingress Aquarius 11:42 AM
Wednesday 21st
Moon ingress Pisces 1:49 AM
Friday 23rd
Mars sextile Neptune 1:39 AM
Mars ingress Aquarius 4:20 AM
Moon ingress Aries 8:25 AM
Sunday 25th
Moon ingress Taurus 1:05 PM
Moon first Quarter at 11:48 PM
Monday 26th
Neptune ingress Aries 2:16 PM
Tuesday 27th
Moon ingress Gemini 3:55 PM
Thursday 29th
Moon ingress Cancer 5:31 PM
Saturday 31st
Moon ingress Leo 7:09 PM

February

Sunday 1st
Full Moon 5:10 PM
Monday 2nd
Moon ingress Virgo 10:21 PM
Tuesday 3rd
Uranus turns direct at 8:53 PM
Thursday 5th
Moon ingress Libra 4:32 AM
Mercury square Uranus 7:13 AM
Friday 6th
Mercury ingress Pisces 5:49 PM
Saturday 7th
Moon ingress Scorpio 2:13 PM
Sunday 8th
Venus Square Uranus 4:48 AM
Monday 9th
Moon last Quarter 7:44 AM
Tuesday 10th
Moon ingress Sagittarius 2:22 AM
Venus ingress Pisces 5:20 AM
Thursday 12th
Mercury opposed South Node 1:17 AM
Moon ingress Capricorn 2:44 PM
Friday 13th
Saturn ingress Aries 7:37 PM
Sunday 15th
Moon ingress Aquarius 1:16 AM

Monday 16th
Sun square Uranus 12:01 AM
Mercury trine Jupiter 4:28 PM
Tuesday 17th
New Moon 7:02 AM
Venus opposed South node 7:45 AM
Moon ingress Pisces 9:09 AM
Wednesday 18th
Sun ingress Pisces 10:54 AM
Thursday 19th
Moon ingress Aries 2:39 PM
Saturday 21st
Moon ingress Taurus 6:31 PM
Sunday 22nd
Venus trine Jupiter 3:01 PM
Monday 23rd
Moon ingress Gemini 9:29 PM
Tuesday 24th
Moon First Quarter 7:28 AM
Thursday 26th
Moon ingress Cancer 12:11 AM
Mercury turns retrograde at 1:47 AM
Friday 27th
Sun opposed South Node 7:32 AM
Mars square Uranus 11:20 AM
Saturday 28th
Moon ingress Leo 3:17 AM

March

Monday 2nd
Moon ingress Virgo 7:34 AM
Mars ingress Pisces 9:19 AM
Tuesday 3rd
Full Moon 6:39 AM
Wednesday 4th
Venus sextile Uranus 11:40 AM
Moon ingress Libra 1:56 PM
Thursday 5th
Sun trine Jupiter 12:13 PM
Friday 6th
Venus ingress Aries 5:47 AM
Moon ingress Scorpio 11:01 PM
Monday 9th
Mercury trine Jupiter 1:22 AM
Moon ingress Sagittarius 11:36 AM
Tuesday 10th
Venus sextile Pluto 2:52 AM
Jupiter turns direct at 11:36 PM
Wednesday 11th
Moon last Quarter at 5:39 AM
Thursday 12th
Moon ingress Capricorn 12:07 AM
Friday 13th
Mars opposed South Node 4:52 PM
Saturday 14th
Moon ingress Aquarius 11:13 AM
Monday 16th
Moon ingress Pisces 7:15 PM
Tuesday 17th
Mercury opposed South Node 5 PM
Wednesday 18th

Venus square Jupiter 12:08 PM
Sun sextile Uranus 4:20 PM
New Moon 9:24 PM
Thursday 19th
Moon ingress Aries 12:03 AM
Friday 20th
Vernal March Equinox 10:47 AM
Sun ingress Aries 10:48 AM
Mercury turns direct at 3:32 PM
Saturday 21st
Moon ingress Taurus 2:35 AM
Mars trine Jupiter 8 PM
Sunday 22nd
Mercury opposed South Node 8:49 PM
Monday 23rd
Moon ingress Gemini 4:18 AM
Wednesday 25th
Moon ingress Cancer 6:33 AM
Sun sextile Pluto 2:16 PM
Moon first Quarter at 3:18 PM
Friday 27th
Moon ingress Leo 10:10 AM
Saturday 28th
Saturn sextile Pluto 6:10 PM
Sunday 29th
Moon ingress Virgo 3:33 PM
Monday 30th
Venus ingress Taurus 12:02 PM
Tuesday 31st
Moon ingress Libra 10:51 PM

April

Wednesday 1st
Full Moon 10:13 PM
Friday 3rd
Mercury trine Jupiter 7:30 AM
Moon ingress Scorpio 8:11 AM
Venus square Pluto 6:38 PM
Sunday 5th
Sun square Jupiter 6:22 PM
Moon ingress Sagittarius 7:31 PM
Monday 6th
Venus sextile North Node 5:47 AM
Venus trine South Node 5:47 AM
Wednesday 8th
Moon ingress Capricorn 8:04 AM
Mars sextile Uranus 12:11 PM
Thursday 9th
Mars ingress Aries 3:39 PM
Friday 10th
Moon last Quarter 12:52 AM
Moon ingress Aquarius 7:55 PM
Monday 13th
Venus sextile Jupiter 4:20 AM
Moon ingress Pisces 4:55 AM
Tuesday 14th
Mercury sextile Uranus 1:11 PM
Mercury ingress Aries 11:23 PM
Wednesday 15th
Moon ingress Aries 10:03 AM
Thursday 16th
Mars sextile Pluto 2:55 PM
Friday 17th
New Moon 7:52 AM

Moon ingress Taurus 11:57 AM
Saturday 18th
Mercury sextile Pluto 4:35 PM
Sunday 19th
Moon ingress Gemini 12:17 PM
Sun ingress Taurus 9:41 PM
Tuesday 21st
Moon ingress Cancer 1:00 PM
Thursday 23rd
Moon ingress Leo 3:41 PM
Moon First Quarter 10:32 PM
Friday 24th
Venus ingress Gemini 12:05 AM
Saturday 25th
Sun square Pluto 12:32 PM
Moon ingress Virgo 9:04 PM
Uranus ingress Gemini 9:35 PM
Sunday 26th
Venus sextile Neptune at 1:42 PM
Mercury Square Jupiter 2:33 PM
Monday 27th
Sun sextile North Node at 9:19 AM
Sun trine South Node at 9:19 AM
Tuesday 28th
Moon ingress Libra 5:03 AM
Venus trine Pluto 12:39 PM
Wednesday 29th
Venus Square North Node at 9:19 PM
Venus Square South Node at 9:19 PM
Thursday 30th
Moon ingress Scorpio 3:02 PM

May

Friday 1st
Full Moon 1:24 PM
Venus sextile Saturn 2:45 PM
Saturday 2nd
Mercury ingress Taurus 10:57 PM
Sunday 3rd
Moon ingress Sagittarius 2:33 AM
Monday 4th
Mars square Jupiter 10:08 PM
Tuesday 5th
Moon ingress Capricorn 3:06 PM
Mercury square Pluto 6:08 PM
Wednesday 6th
Mercury sextile North Node 2:06 AM
Mercury South Node 2:06 AM
Pluto turns retrograde at 10:14 AM
Friday 8th
Moon ingress Aquarius 3:27 AM
Saturday 9th
Moon Last Quarter 5:11 PM
Sunday 10th
Moon ingress Pisces 1:39 PM
Sun sextile Jupiter 10:13 PM
Tuesday 12th
Moon ingress Aries 8:03 PM
Wednesday 13th
Mercury sextile Jupiter 12:43 AM
Thursday 14th
Moon ingress Taurus 10:31 PM
Saturday 16th New Moon 4:02 PM
Moon ingress Gemini 10:23 PM
Sunday 17th
Mercury ingress Gemini 6:27 AM

Monday 18th
Mars ingress Taurus 6:28 PM
Venus ingress Cancer 9:07 PM
Moon ingress Cancer 9:46 PM
Tuesday 19th
Mercury sextile Neptune 12:04 AM
Venus sextile Mars 1:37 AM
Mercury Square North Node 12 PM
Mercury Square South Node 12 PM
Mercury trine Pluto 6:52 PM
Wednesday 20th
Sun ingress Gemini 8:39 PM
Moon ingress Leo 10:48 PM
Friday 22nd
Venus square Neptune 2:31 AM
Mercury sextile Saturn 2:02 PM
Venus trine North node 5:55 PM
Venus sextile South node 5:55 PM
Saturday 23rd
Moon ingress Virgo 2:57 AM
Moon First Quarter 7:12 AM
Sunday 24th
Mars sextile North Node 9:56 PM
Mars trine South Node 9:56 PM
Sun sextile Neptune 10:22 PM
Monday 25th
Moon ingress Libra 10:34 AM
Sun square North node 3:22 PM
Sun square South node 3:22 PM
Tuesday 26th
Mars square Pluto 12:01 AM
Sun trine Pluto 11:52 AM
Wednesday 27th
Moon ingress Scorpio 8:52 PM
Thursday 28th
Venus square Saturn at 11:02 PM

Saturday 30th
Moon ingress Sagittarius 8:45 AM

Sunday 31st
Full Moon 4:46 AM

June

Monday 1st
Mercury ingress Cancer 7:57 AM
Moon ingress Capricorn 9:19 PM
Tuesday 2nd
Sun sextile Saturn 6:48 PM
Wednesday 3rd
Mercury trine North Node 7:39 AM
Mercury sextile South Node 7:39 AM
Mercury Square Neptune 8:17 PM
Thursday 4th
Moon ingress Aquarius 9:45 AM
Saturday 6th
Moon ingress Pisces 8:42 PM
Monday 8th
Moon last Quarter 6:01 AM
Tuesday 9th
Moon ingress Aries 4:33 AM
Wednesday 10th
Mercury square Saturn 1:37 AM
Thursday 11th
Moon ingress Taurus 8:27 AM
Friday 12th
Uranus square North Node 2:43 PM
Uranus square South Node 2:43 PM
Saturday 13th
Venus ingress Leo 6:49 AM
Moon ingress Gemini 9:06 AM
Sunday 14th
New Moon 10:55 PM
Monday 15th
Moon ingress Cancer 8:14 AM
Venus sex tile Uranus 6:52 PM

Tuesday 16th
Venus trine Neptune at 11:40 PM
Wednesday 17th
Moon ingress Leo 8:05 AM
Venus opposed to Pluto 4:38 PM
Friday 19th
Moon ingress Virgo 10:37 AM
Sunday 21st
June Solstice 4:25 AM
Sun ingress Cancer 4:27 AM
Moon ingress Libra 4:55 PM
Moon first Quarter at 5:56 PM
Tuesday 23rd
Sun trine North node 2:09 AM
Sun sextile South node 2:09 AM
Wednesday 24th
Moon ingress Scorpio 2:43 AM
Thursday 25th
Venus trine Saturn 8:01 AM
Sun square Neptune 6:38 PM
Friday 26th
Moon ingress Sagittarius 2:41 PM
Sunday 28th
Mars sextile Jupiter 12:50 AM
Mars ingress Gemini 3:33 PM
Monday 29th
Moon ingress Capricorn 3:18 AM
Mercury turns retrograde at 1:35 PM
full Moon 7:57 PM
Tuesday 30th
Mars square North node 1:31 AM
Mars square South node 1:31 AM
Jupiter ingress Leo 2:07 AM

July

Wednesday 1st
Moon ingress Aquarius 3:33 PM
Saturday 4th
Moon ingress Pisces 2:30 AM
Mars sextile Neptune 8:44 PM
Sunday 5th
Mars trine Pluto 9:06 AM
Monday 6th
Sun square Saturn 6:47 AM
Moon ingress Aries 11:07 AM
Tuesday 7th
Neptune turns retro at 7:40 AM
Moon last Quarter 3:30 PM
Wednesday 8th
Moon ingress Taurus 4:30 PM
Thursday 9th
Venus ingress Virgo 1:25 PM
Friday 10th
Venus opposed North Node 4:20 AM
Moon ingress Gemini 6:41 PM
Sunday 12th
Moon ingress Cancer 6:46 PM
Monday 13th
Venus Square Uranus 10:26 AM
Tuesday 14th
New Moon 5:44 AM
Moon ingress Leo 6:35 PM
Wednesday 15th
Uranus sextile Neptune 4:35 PM
Thursday 16th
Moon ingress Virgo 8:07 PM
Saturday 18th
Uranus trine Pluto 12:43 AM

Sunday 19th
Moon ingress Libra 12:57 AM
Mars sextile Saturn 2:10 PM
Monday 20th
Jupiter trine Neptune 3:23 AM
Jupiter opposed Pluto at 10:44 AM
Tuesday 21st
Moon First Quarter 7:06 AM
Jupiter sextile Uranus 7:10 AM
Moon ingress Scorpio 9:35 AM
Wednesday 22nd
Sun ingress Leo 3:16 PM
Thursday 23rd
Mercury turns direct at 6:58 PM
Sagittarius 9:07 PM
Friday 24th
Mercury sextile Venus 12:08 PM
Saturday 25th
Neptune sextile Pluto 1:25 AM
Sunday 26th
Moon ingress Capricorn 9:44 AM
Saturn turns retrograde at 3:29 PM
Nth Node ingress Aquarius 9:02 PM
South Node ingress Leo 9:02 PM
Monday 27th
Sun opposed Pluto at 2:55 AM
Sun trine Neptune 3:36 AM
Sun sextile Uranus 5:36 PM
Tuesday 28th
Moon ingress Aquarius 9:46 PM
Wednesday 29th
Venus square Mars 3:09 AM
Full Moon 10:36 AM
Friday 31st
Moon ingress Pisces 8:14 AM

August

Sunday 2nd
Moon ingress Aries 4:36 PM
Tuesday 4th
Moon ingress Taurus 10:35 PM
Wednesday 5th
Moon last Quarter at 10:22 PM
Thursday 6th
Venus ingress Libra 3:16 PM
Sun trine Saturn 10:44 PM
Friday 7th
Moon ingress Gemini 2:07 AM
Sunday 9th
Moon ingress Cancer 3:45 AM
Mercury ingress Leo 12:30 PM
Monday 10th
Venus trine Pluto 2:08 PM
Venus opposed Neptune 6:01 PM
Mars sextile South Node 11:38 PM
Mars trine North Node 11:38 PM
Tuesday 11th
Mars ingress Cancer 4:36 AM
Moon ingress Leo 4:38 AM
Mercury opposed Pluto 9:20 PM
Mercury trine Neptune at 11:40 PM
Venus trine Uranus at 11:45 PM
Wednesday 12th
New Moon 1:37 PM
Mercury sextile Uranus 4:49 PM
Thursday 13th
Moon ingress Virgo 6:18 AM
Mercury sextile Venus 12:25 PM
Saturday 15th
Mercury conjunct Jupiter 7:23 AM
Moon ingress Libra 10:20 AM

Monday 17th
Mars square Neptune 5:52 AM
Mercury trine Saturn 11:27 AM
Venus sextile Jupiter 12:15 PM
Moon ingress Scorpio 5:46 PM
Wednesday 19th
Moon First Quarter at 10:47 PM
Thursday 20th
Moon ingress Sagittarius 4:30 AM
Friday 21st
Venus opposed Saturn 8:42 AM
Saturday 22nd
Moon ingress Capricorn 4:59 PM
Sun opposed North Node 8 PM
Sun conjunct South Node 8 PM
Sun ingress Virgo 10:22 PM
Tuesday 25th
Moon ingress Aquarius 5:01 AM
Mercury opposed North Node 6:10 AM
Mercury conjunct South Node 6:10 AM
Mercury ingress Virgo 7:06 AM
Thursday 27th
Sun conjunct Mercury 1:03 PM
Moon ingress Pisces 3:03 PM
Friday 28th
Full Moon 12:19 AM
Mercury square Uranus 3:24 AM
Sun square Uranus 6:18 PM
Saturday 29th
Moon ingress Aries 10:37 PM
Monday 31st
Jupiter trine Saturn 6:17 PM

September

Tuesday 1st
Moon ingress Taurus 4:01 AM
Mars square Saturn at 5:58 AM
Mercury sextile Mars 9:20 AM
Thursday 3rd
Moon ingress Gemini 7:47 AM
Friday 4th
Moon Last Quarter 3:52 AM
Saturday 5th
Moon ingress Cancer 10:30 AM
Monday 7th
Moon ingress Leo 12:49 PM
Wednesday 9th
Moon ingress Virgo 3:35 PM
Thursday 10th
Venus trine North Node 2:07 AM
Venus sextile South Node 2:07 AM
Venus ingress Scorpio 4:12 AM
Mercury ingress Libra 12:22 PM
Uranus turns retrograde at 3:29 PM
New Moon 11:28 PM
Friday 11th
Moon ingress Libra 7:52 PM
Saturday 12th
Mercury trine Pluto 11:58 AM
Mercury opposed Neptune at 12:37 PM
Sunday 13th
Mercury trine Uranus 10:39 PM
Monday 14th
Moon ingress Scorpio 2:44 AM
Black Moon ingress Capricorn 1:37 PM
Sun sextile Mars 3:53 PM

Tuesday 15th
Venus square Pluto 2:33 PM
Neptune sextile Pluto 10:10 PM
Wednesday 16th
Moon ingress Sagittarius 12:41 PM
Friday 18th
Mercury opposed Saturn at 6 AM
Moon First Quarter 4:44 PM
Saturday 19th
Moon ingress Capricorn 12:55 AM
Monday 21st
Moon ingress Aquarius 1:14 PM
Mercury sextile Jupiter 6:50 PM
Tuesday 22nd
September Equinox 8:06 PM
Sun ingress Libra 8:08 PM
Wednesday 23rd
Moon ingress Pisces 11:23 PM
Friday 25th
Sun opposed Neptune 9:36 PM
Saturday 26th
Sun trine Pluto 1:34 AM
Moon ingress Aries 6:23 AM
Full Moon 12:50 PM
Sunday 27th
Mars ingress Leo 10:54 PM
Monday 28th
Moon ingress Taurus 10:40 AM
Sun trine Uranus 12:21 PM
Tuesday 29th
Mercury trine North Node 6:03 PM
Mercury sextile South Node 6:03 PM
Wednesday 30th
Mercury ingress Scorpio 7:47 AM
Moon ingress Gemini 1:26 P

October

Friday 2nd
Mercury square Mars 5:13 AM
Moon ingress Cancer 3:54 PM
Mercury square Pluto 4:42 PM
Mars trine Neptune 6:17 PM
Saturday 3rd
Venus turns retrograde at 3:14 AM
Mars opposed Pluto 6:38 AM
Moon Last Quarter 9:26 AM
Sunday 4th
Sun opposed Saturn 8:29 AM
Moon ingress Leo 6:54 PM
Tuesday 6th
Mercury conjunct Venus 8:10 PM
Moon ingress Virgo 10:52 PM
Wednesday 7th
Mars sextile Uranus 6:41 AM
Friday 9th
Moon ingress Libra 4:10 AM
Saturday 10th
new Moon 11:51 AM
Venus square Mars 5:32 PM
Sunday 11th
Moon ingress Scorpio 11:21 AM
Tuesday 13th
Moon ingress Sagittarius 8:59 PM
Thursday 15th
Sun sextile Jupiter 4:21 AM
Pluto turns direct at 11:36 PM
Friday 16th
Mars trine Saturn 4:32 AM

Moon ingress Capricorn 5:57 AM
Sunday 18th
Moon First Quarter 12:13 PM
Moon ingress Aquarius 9:40 PM
Tuesday 20th
Venus square Pluto at 2:57 AM
Wednesday 21st
Sun trine North Node 6:34 AM
Sun sextile South Node 6:34 AM
Moon ingress Pisces 8:35 AM
Friday 23rd
Sun ingress Scorpio 5:41 AM
Moon ingress Aries 5:53 PM
Sun conjunct Venus 11:44 PM
Saturday 24th
Mercury turns retrograde at 3:13 AM
Sunday 25th
Venus ingress Libra 5:04 AM
Moon ingress Taurus 7:34 PM
Monday 26th
Full Moon 12:12 AM
Sun square Pluto 8:11 AM
Tuesday 27th
Moon ingress Gemini 9:02 PM
Thursday 29th
Moon ingress Cancer 10:05 PM
Friday 30th
Mercury square Mars 1:23 PM
Venus trine North Node 6:13 PM
Venus sextile South Node 6:13 PM

November

Sunday 1st
Moon ingress Leo 12:18 AM
Moon last Quarter 3:29 PM
Tuesday 3rd
Moon ingress Virgo 3:28 AM
Wednesday 4th
Venus sextile Jupiter 5:28 AM
Sun conjunct Mercury 9:24 AM
Thursday 5th
Moon ingress Libra 9:38 AM
Saturday 7th
Moon ingress Scorpio 5:40 PM
Monday 9th
New Moon 2:03 AM
Tuesday 10th
Venus sextile Mars 1:45 AM
Moon ingress Sagittarius 3:36 AM
Thursday 12th
Jupiter opposed North Node 12:13 AM
Jupiter conjunct South Node 12:13 AM
Moon ingress Capricorn 3:27 PM
Friday 13th
Mercury turns direct at 10:54 AM
Venus turns direct at 7:28 PM
Saturday 14th
Mars opposed North Node 2:57 PM
Mars conjunct South Node 2:57 PM
Sunday 15th
Moon ingress Aquarius 4:24 AM
Monday 16th
Mars conjunct Jupiter at 1:23 AM

Tuesday 17th
Moon First Quarter 6:49 AM
Sun square North Node 8:13 AM
Sun square South Node 8:13 AM
Moon ingress Pisces 4:19 PM
Wednesday 18th
Sun square Jupiter 4:38 AM
Thursday 19th
Sun square Mars 12:49 PM
Friday 20th
Moon ingress Aries 12:52 AM
Sunday 22nd
Sun ingress Sagittarius 2:26 AM
Moon ingress Taurus 5:09 AM
Monday 23rd
Venus trine North Node 7:33 AM
Venus sextile South Node 7:33 AM
Sun trine Neptune 7:07 PM
Tuesday 24th
Moon ingress Gemini 6:09 AM
Full Moon 9:54 AM
Wednesday 25th
Sun sextile Pluto 12:27 PM
Sun opposed Uranus 5:41 PM
Mars ingress Virgo 6:45 PM
Thursday 26th
Moon ingress Cancer 5:51 AM
Saturday 28th
Moon ingress Leo 6:20 AM
Venus sex tile Jupiter 7:07 AM
Sunday 29th
Uranus trine Pluto 6:23 AM
Monday 30th
Sun trine Saturn 1:05 AM
Moon ingress Virgo 9:13 AM

December

Tuesday 1st
Moon last Quarter 1:09 AM
Mercury square North node 10:06 PM
Mercury square South node 10:06 PM
Wednesday 2nd
Moon ingress Libra 3:04 PM
Friday 4th
Mercury square Jupiter 2:02 AM
Venus ingress Scorpio 3:17 AM
Mars square Uranus 2:27 PM
Moon ingress Scorpio 11:35 PM
Sunday 5th
Mercury ingress Sagittarius 3:35 AM
Monday 7th
Mercury trine Neptune 5:15 AM
Moon ingress Sagittarius 10:06 AM
Tuesday 8th
Mercury opposed Uranus 5:29 AM
Mercury sextile Pluto 2:31 PM
New Moon 7:53 PM
Wednesday 9th
Mercury square Mars 8:40 AM
Venus square Pluto 1:38 PM
Moon ingress Capricorn 10:09 PM
Thursday 10th
Saturn turns direct at 7 PM
Friday 11th
Mercury trine Saturn 8:25 AM
Saturday 12th
Venus sextile Mars 4:16 a.m.
Moon ingress Aquarius 11:05 AM

Neptune turns direct at 6:11 PM
Jupiter turns retrograde at 7:47 PM
Monday 14th
Sun sextile North Node 3:59 AM
Sun trine South Node 3:59 AM
Moon ingress Pisces 11:35 PM
Thursday 17th
Moon First Quarter 12:43 AM
Moon ingress Aries 9:34 AM
Friday 18th
Sun trine Jupiter 4:21 PM
Saturday 19th
Moon ingress Taurus 3:29 PM
Sunday 20th
Mercury sextile North Node 12:31 PM
Mercury trine South Node 12:31 PM
Monday 21st
December Solstice 3:51 PM
Sun ingress Capricorn 3:54 PM
Moon ingress Gemini 5:27 PM
Wednesday 23rd
Sun square Neptune 6:37 AM
Mercury trine Jupiter 1:03 PM
Moon ingress Cancer 4:58 PM
Full Moon 8:29 PM
Friday 25th
Mercury ingress Capricorn 1:25 PM
Moon ingress Leo 4:12 PM
Saturday 26th
Mercury square Neptune 2:46 PM
Sunday 27th
Moon ingress Virgo 5:13 PM
Tuesday 29th
Venus square North Node 4:42 PM

Venus square South Node 4:42 PM
Sun square Saturn 6:27 PM
Moon ingress Libra 9:27 PM
Wednesday 30th
Moon last Quarter 2 PM

Mercury square Saturn 6:54 PM
Thursday 31st
Sun trine Mars 7:03 AM
Mercury trine Mars 6:30 PM

Astrology, Tarot & Horoscope Books.

Mystic Cat